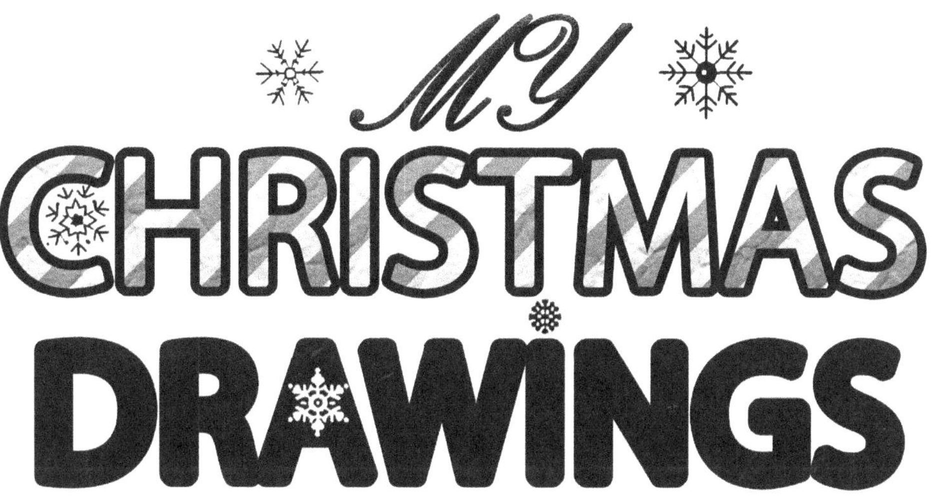
MY
CHRISTMAS
DRAWINGS

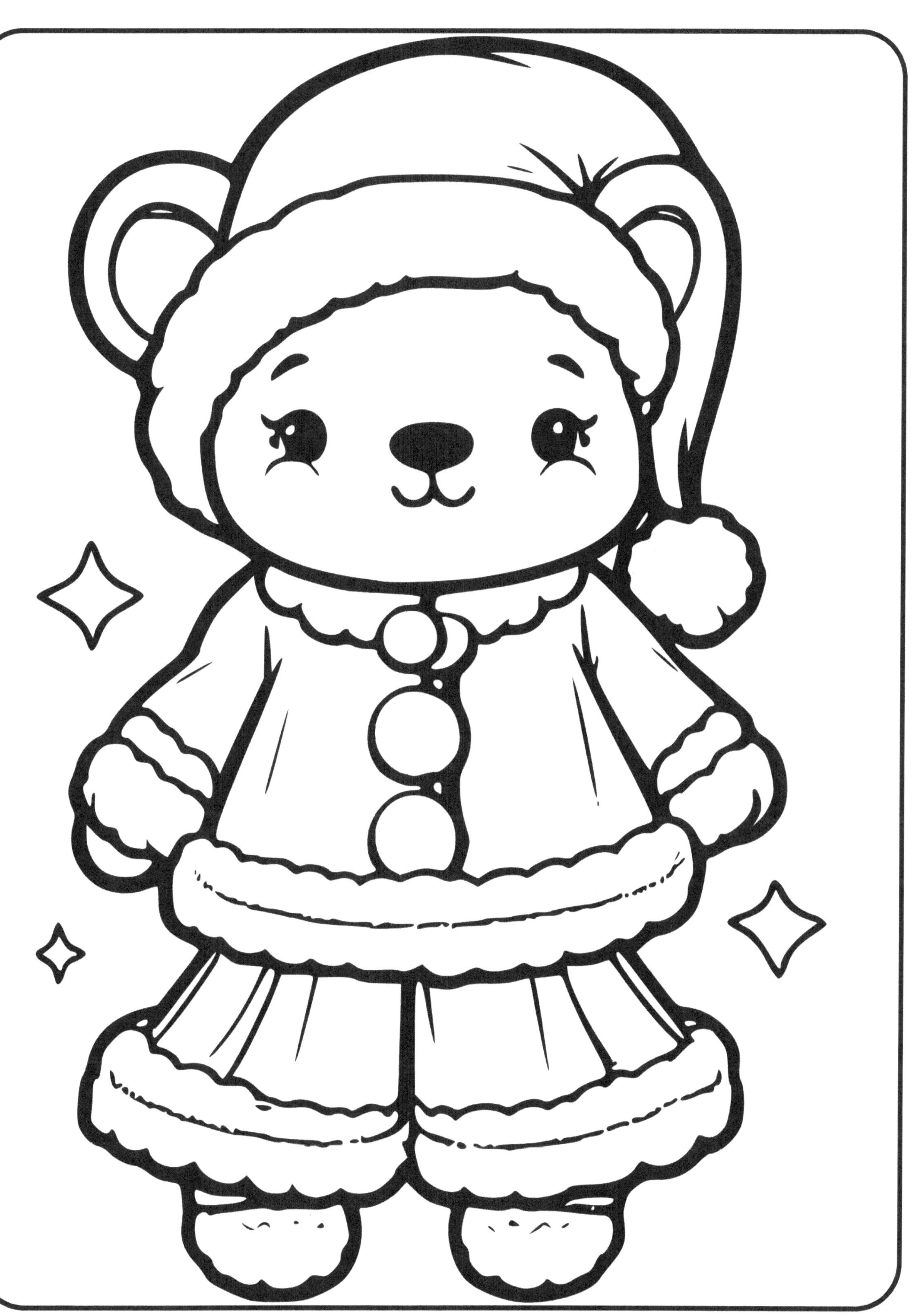

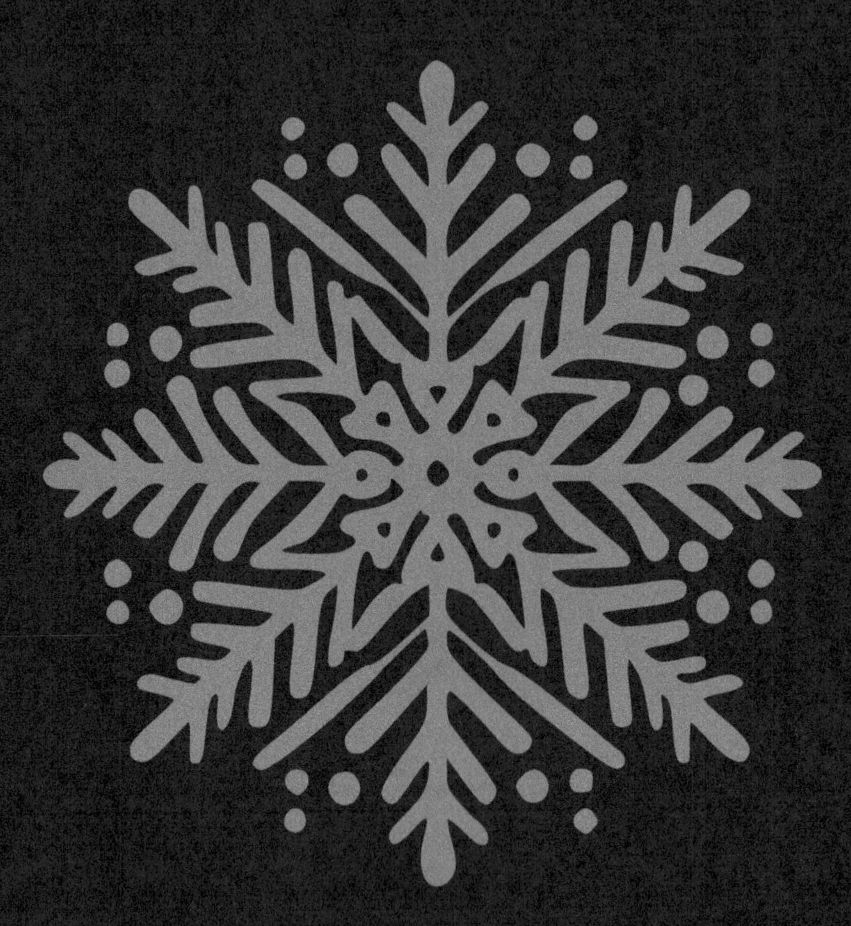

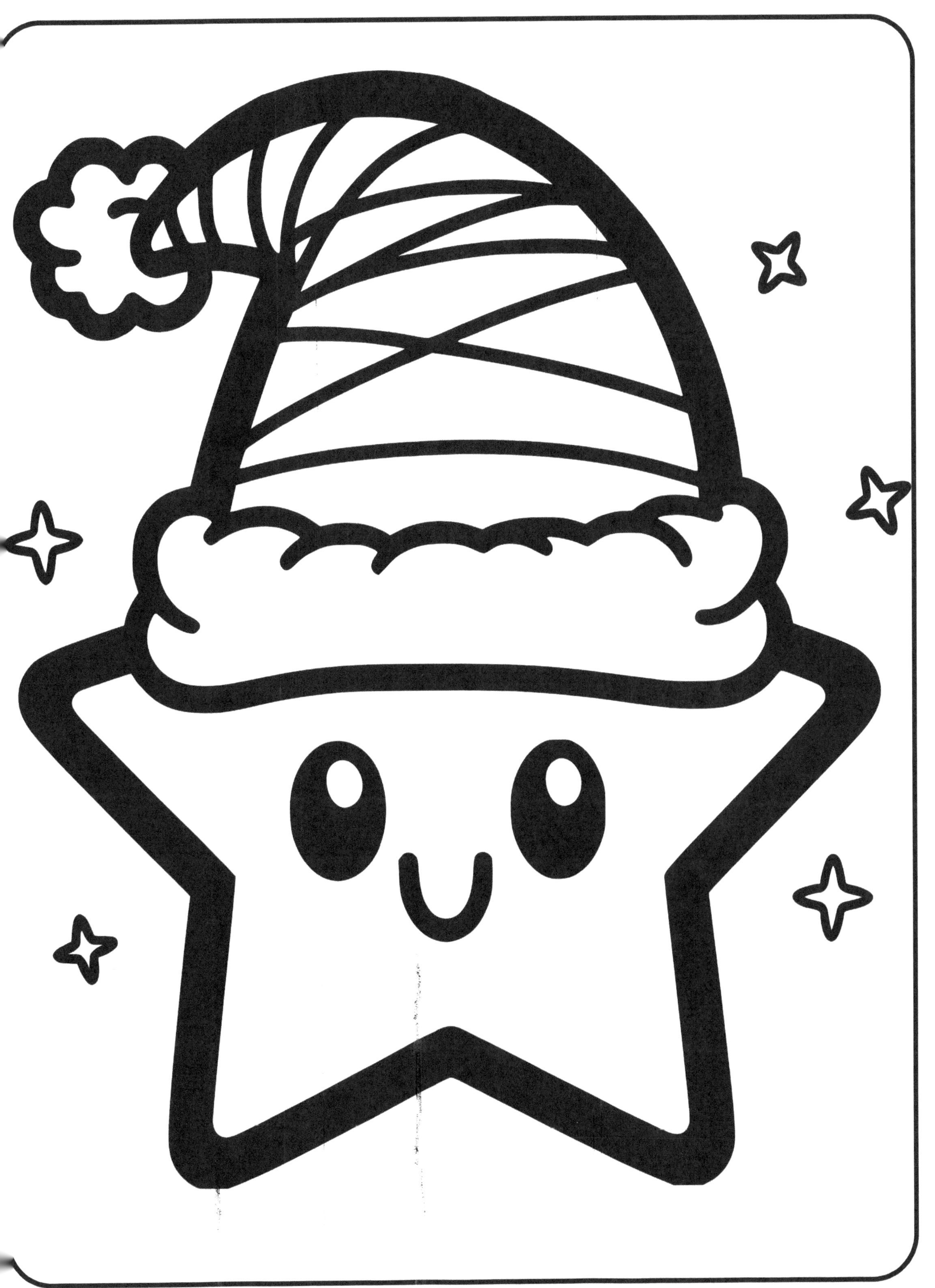

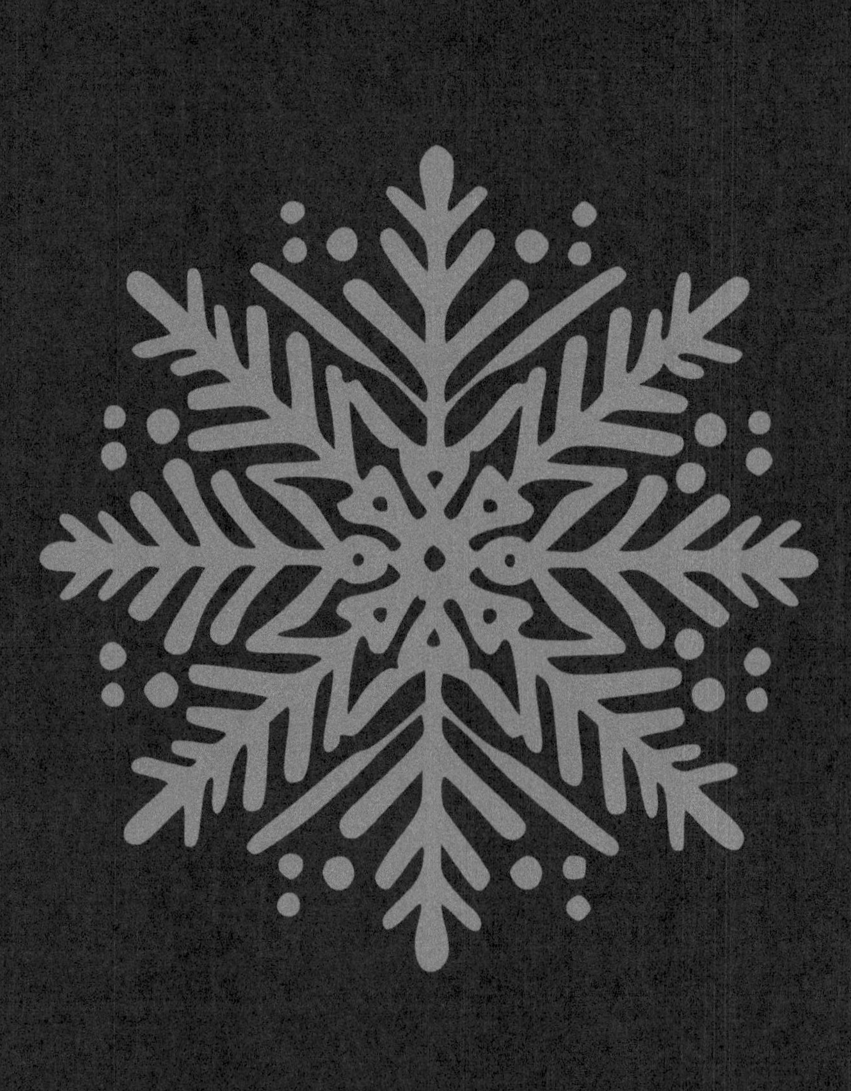

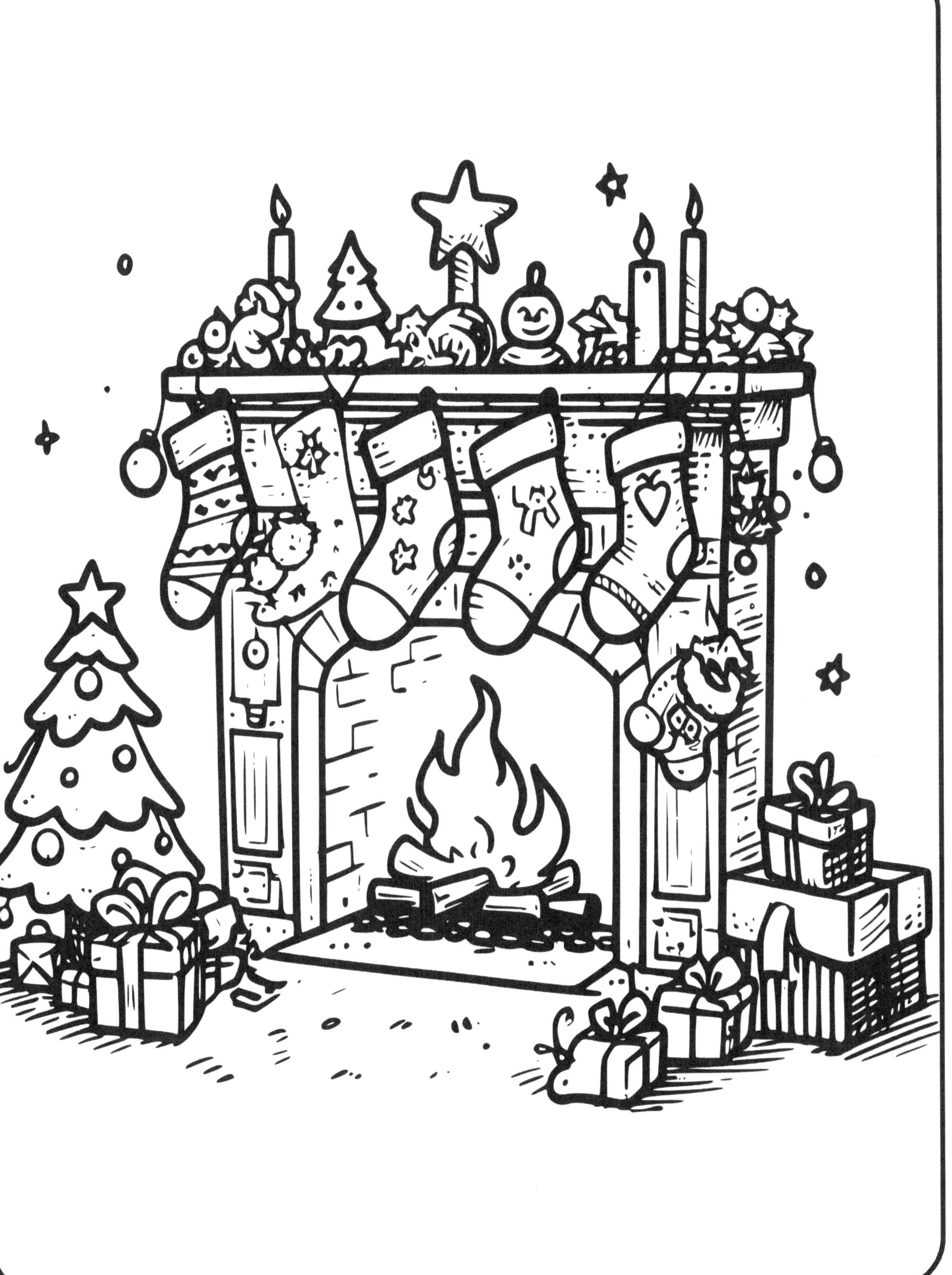

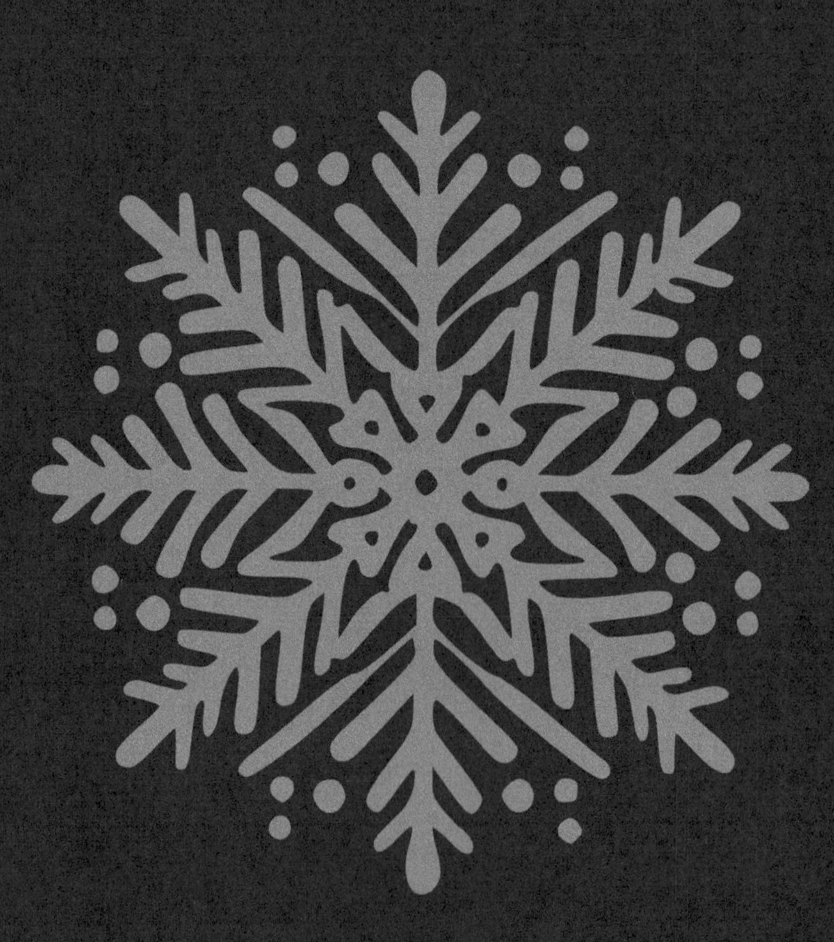

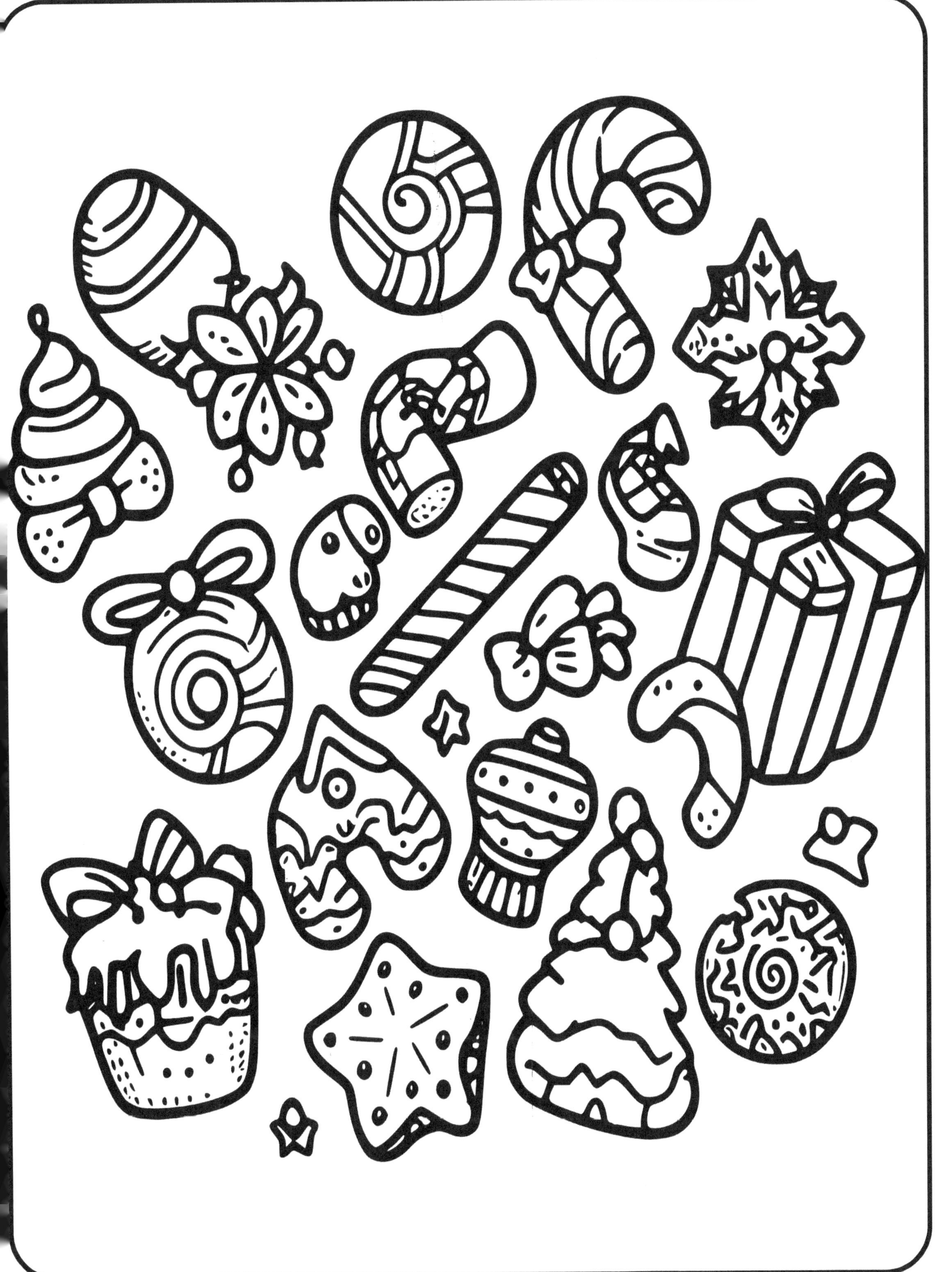

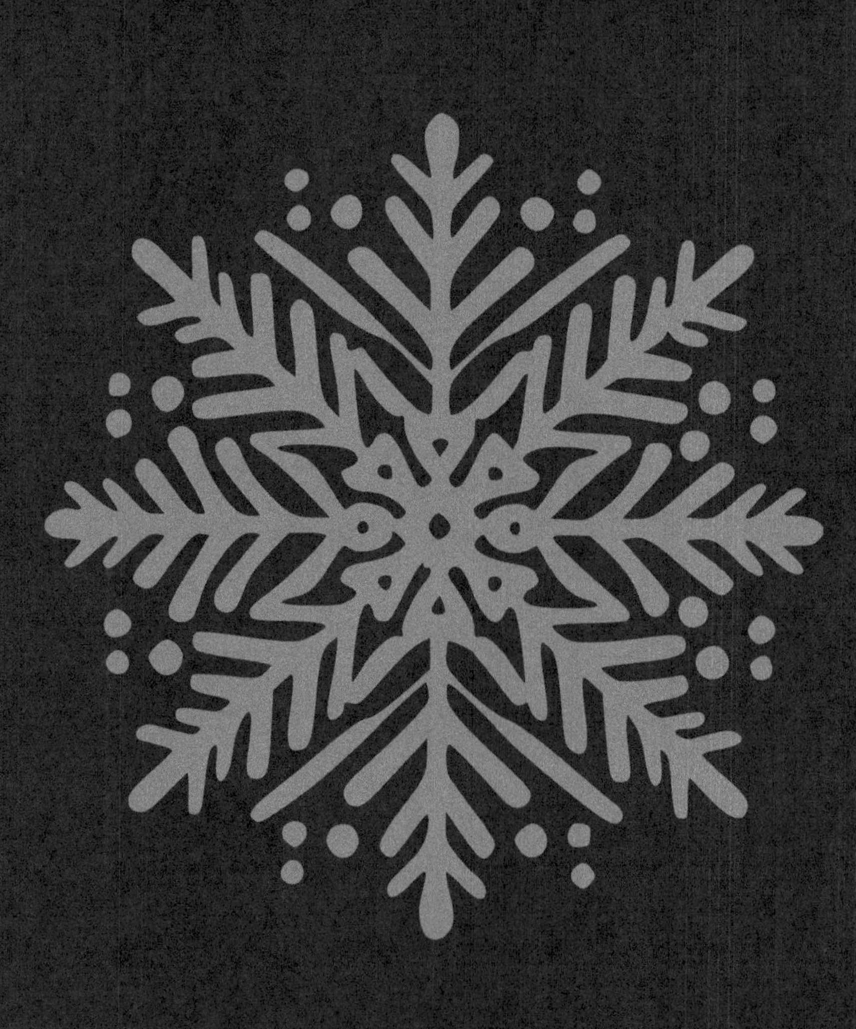

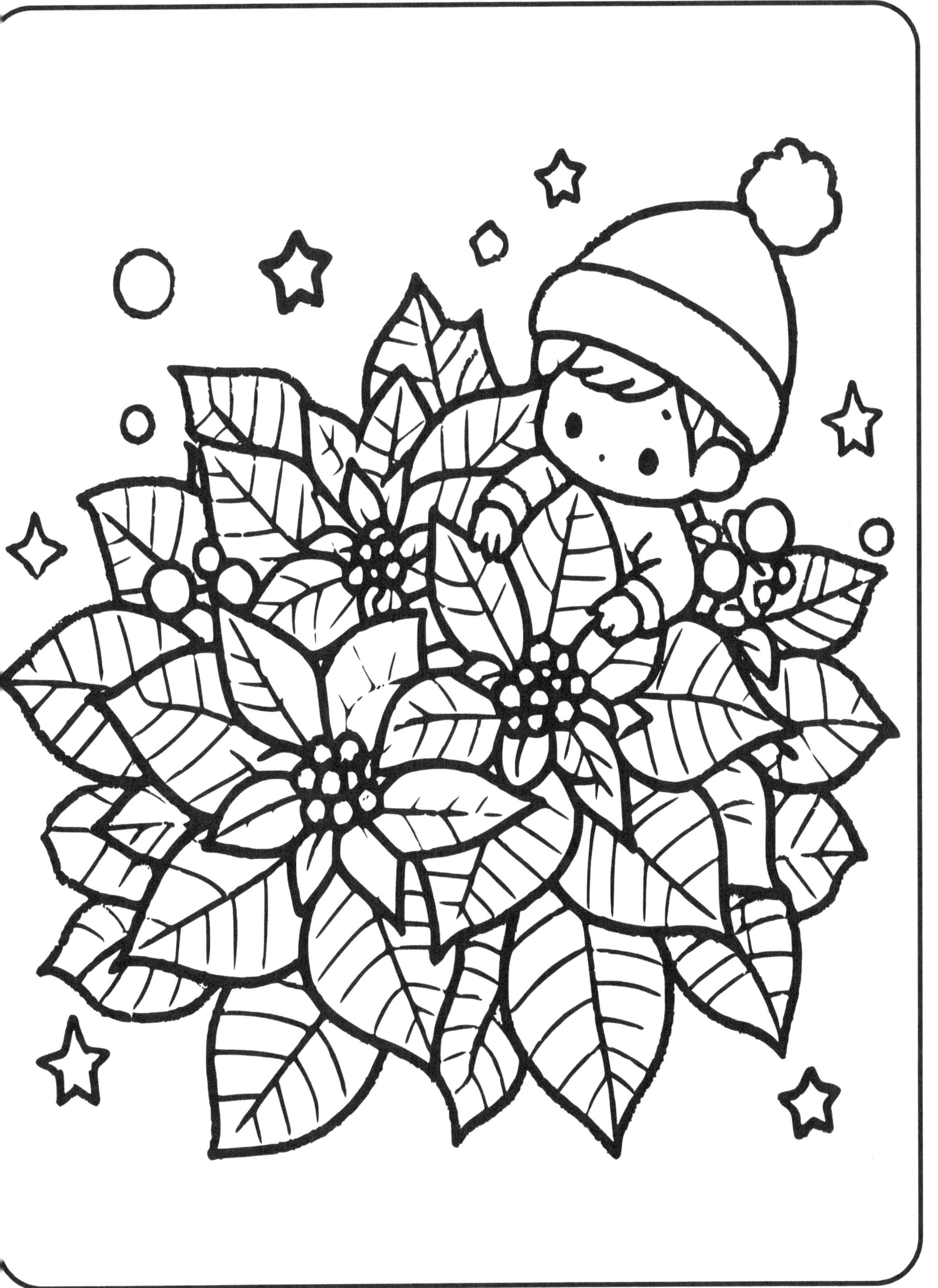

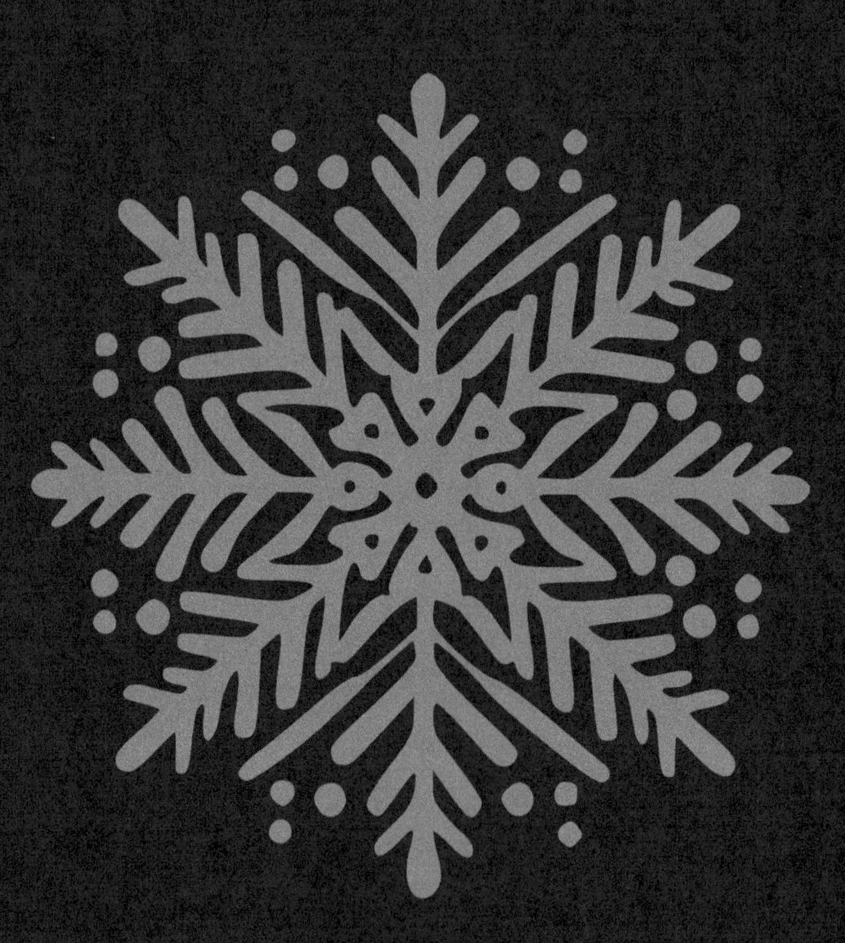

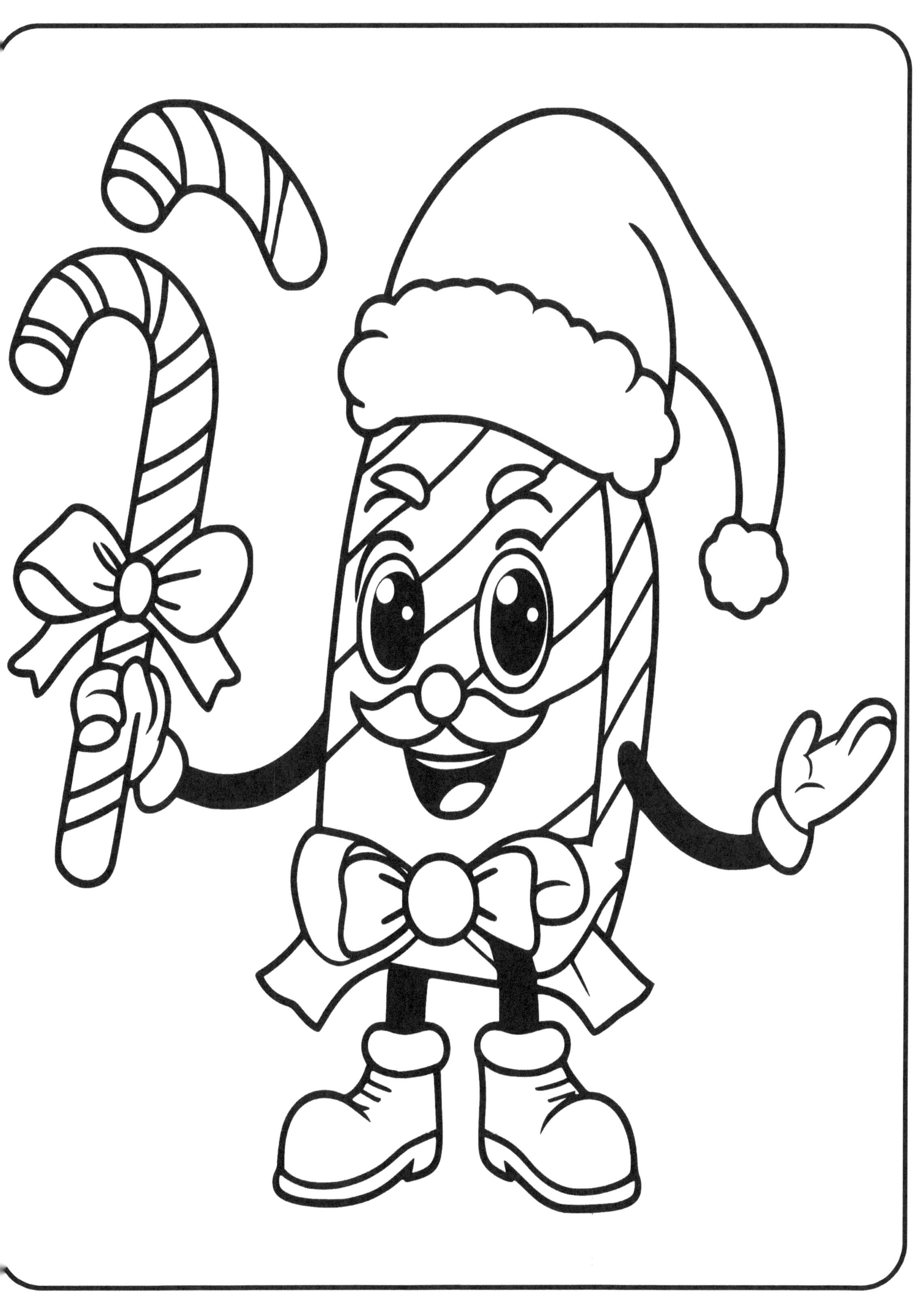

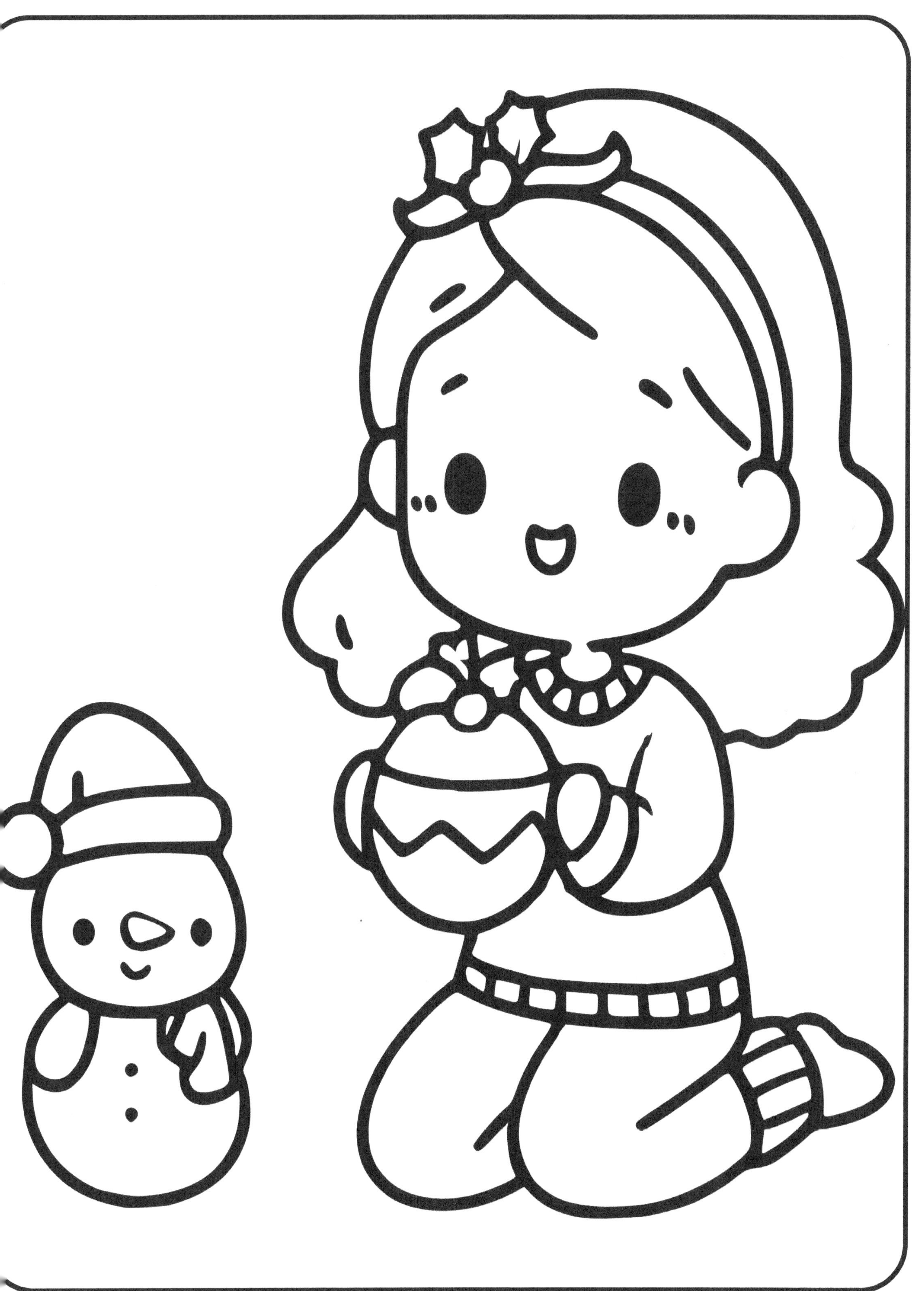

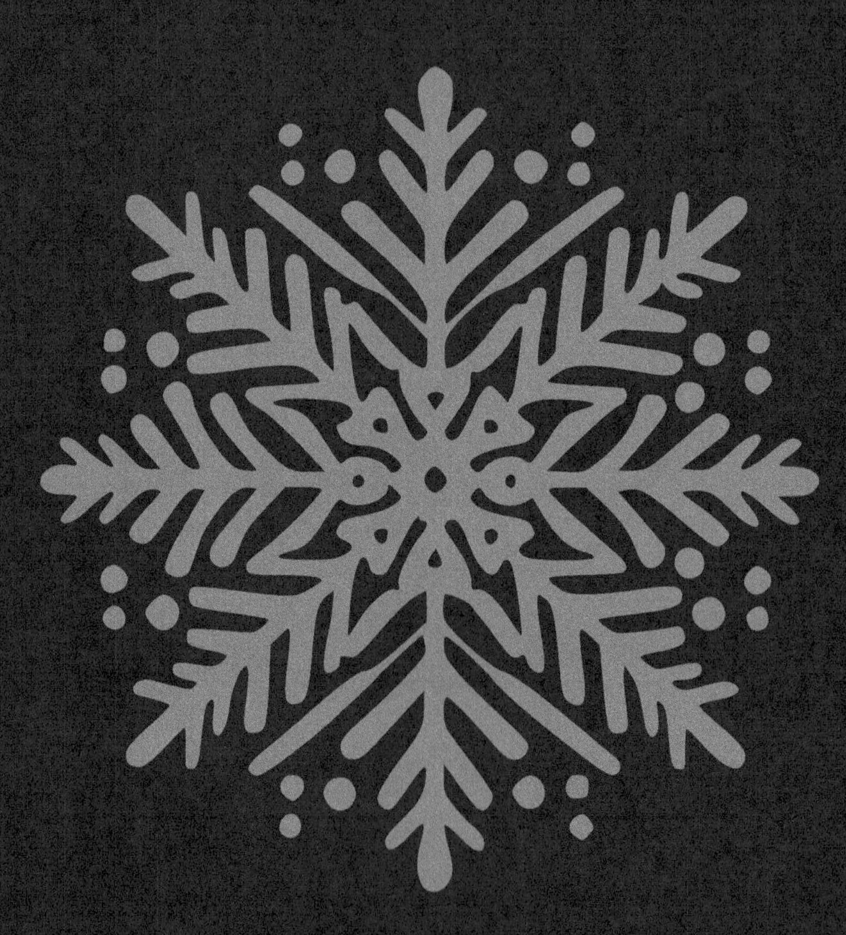

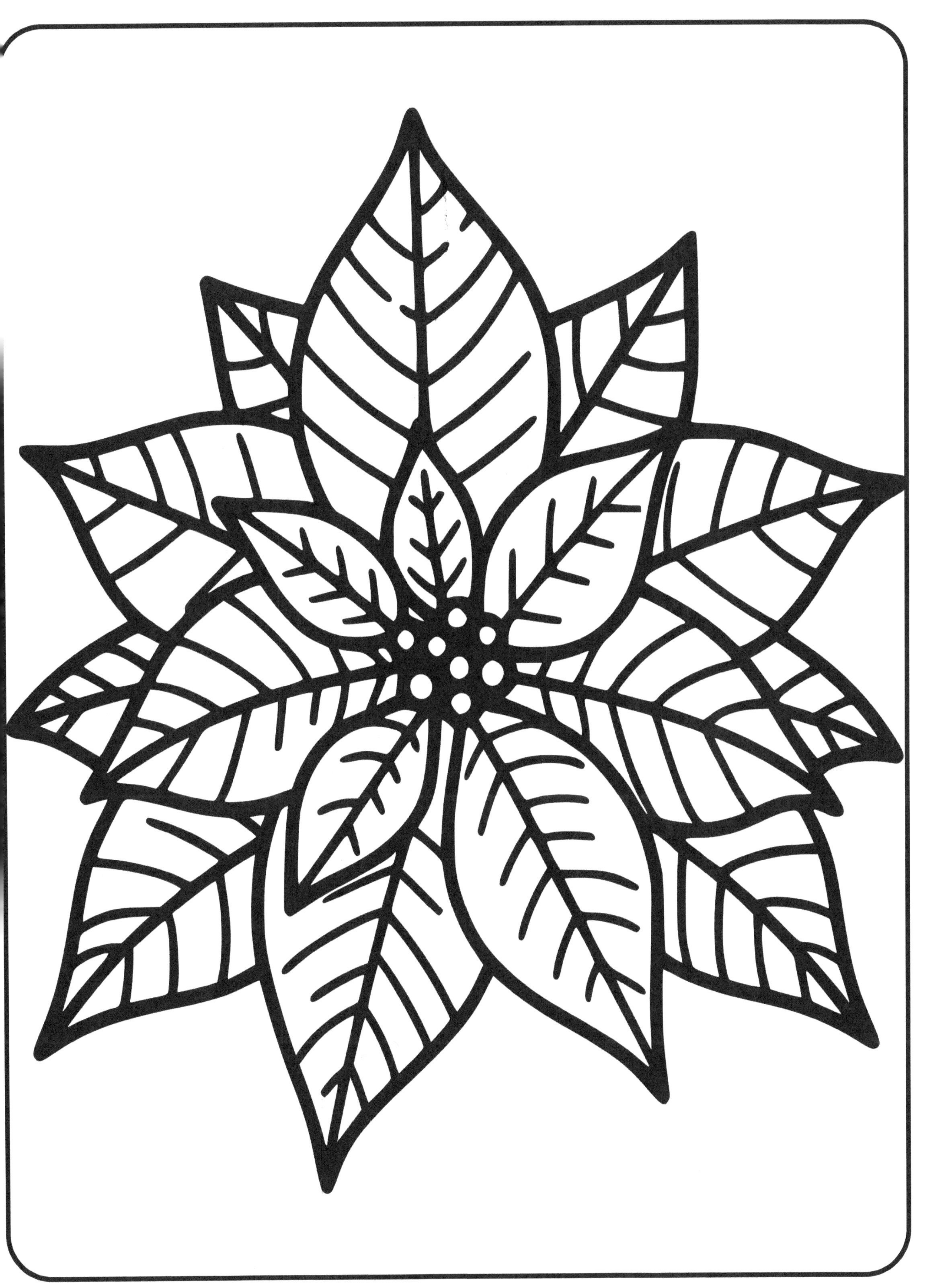

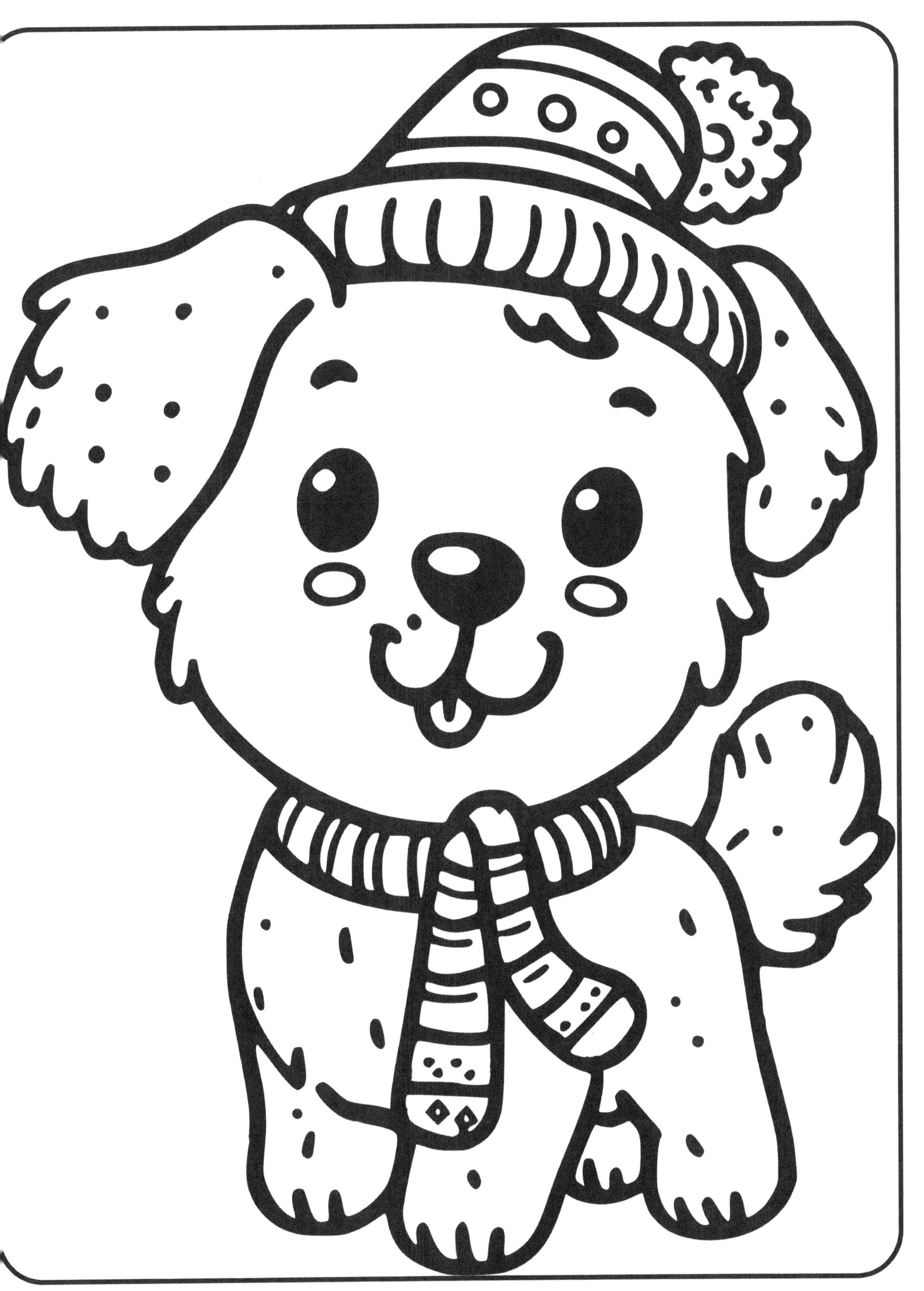

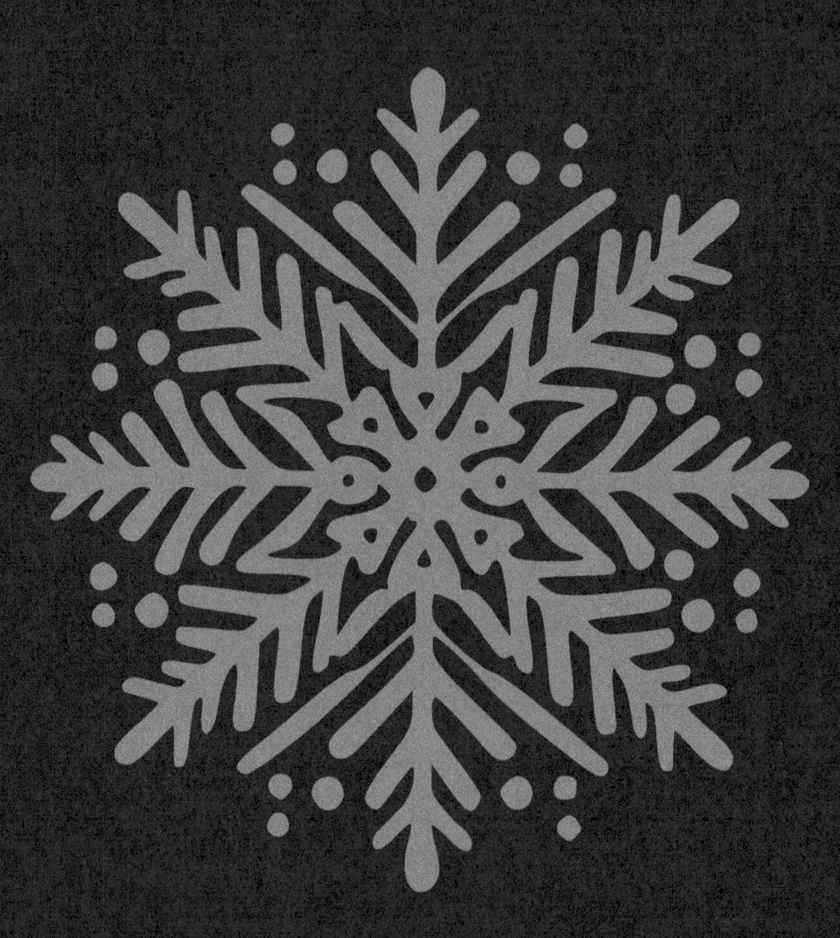

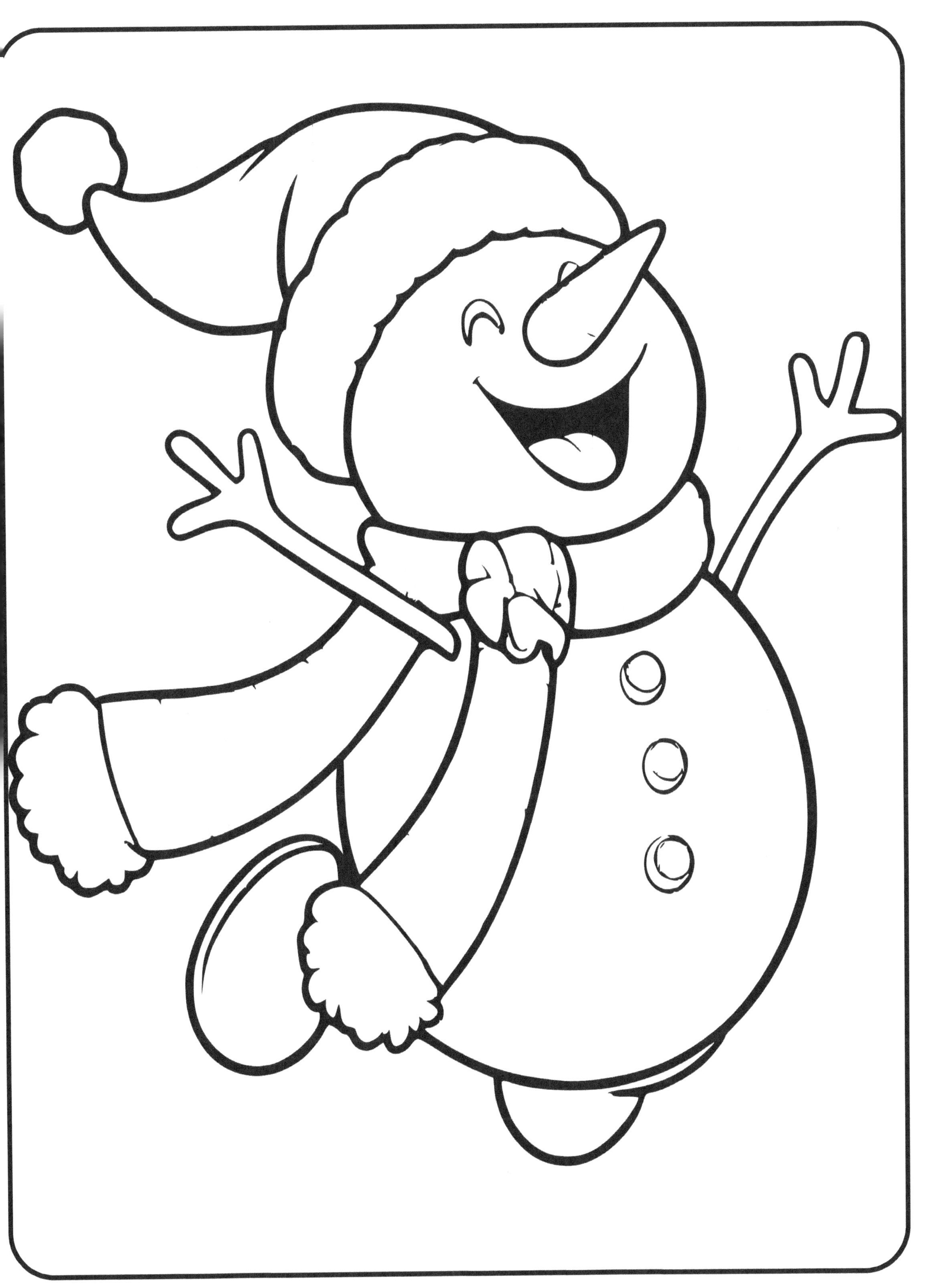

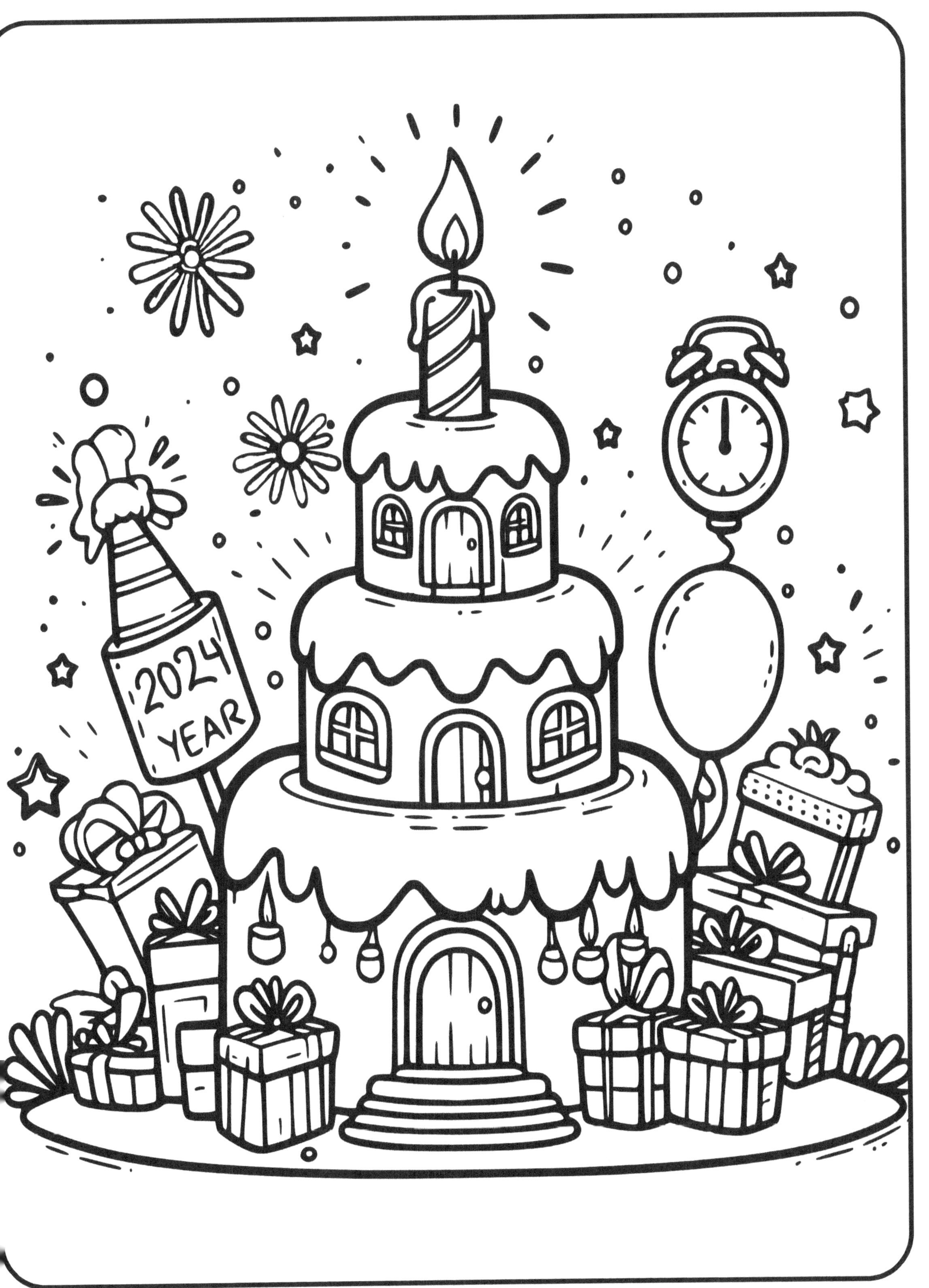

2024
YEAR

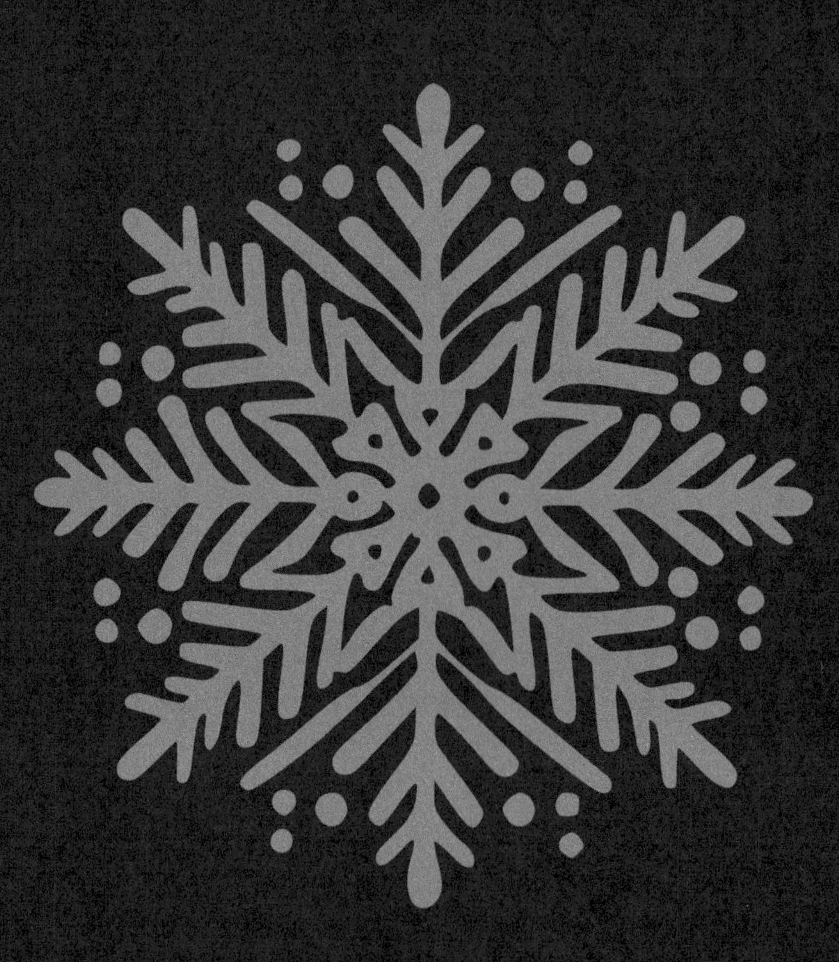

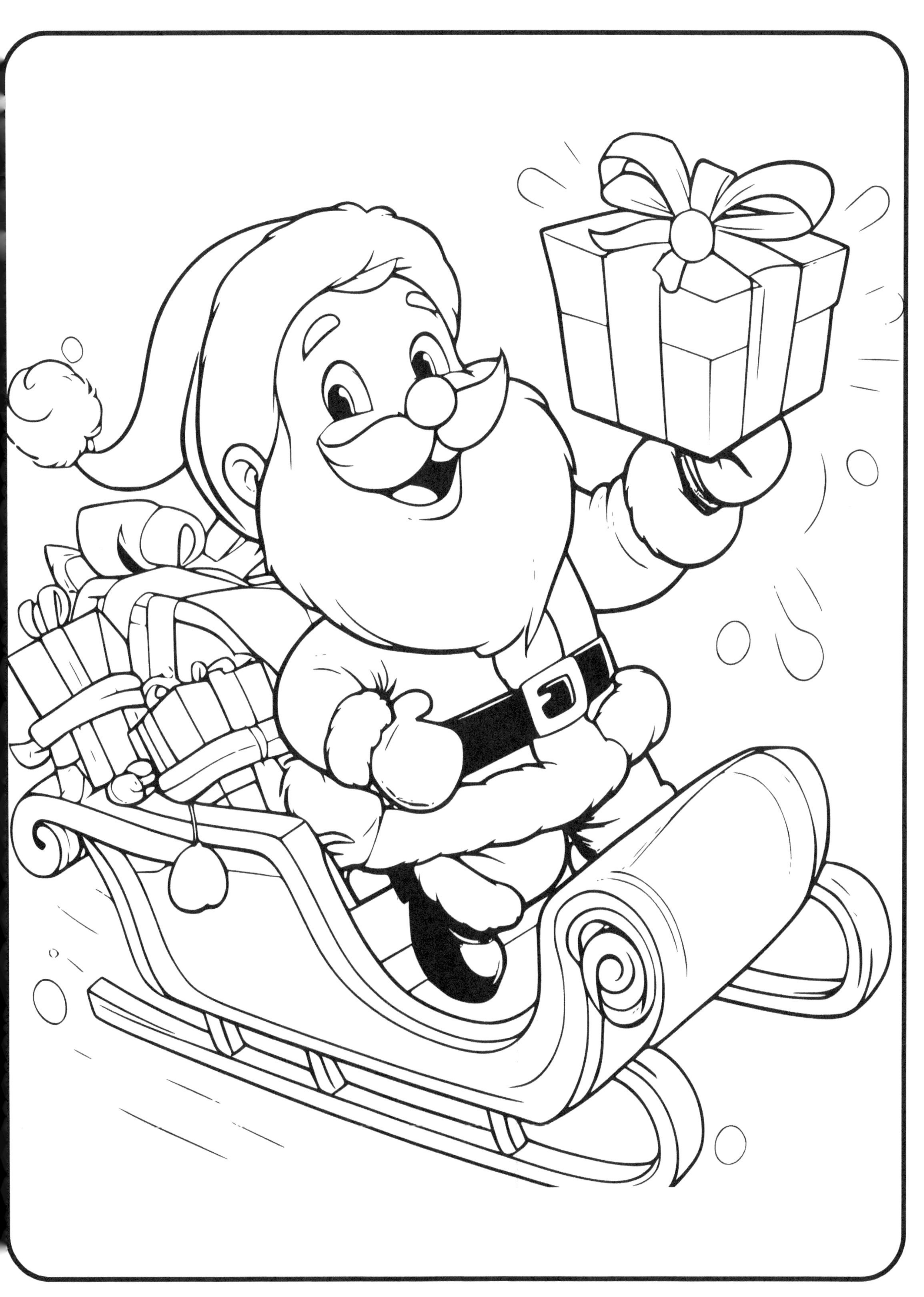

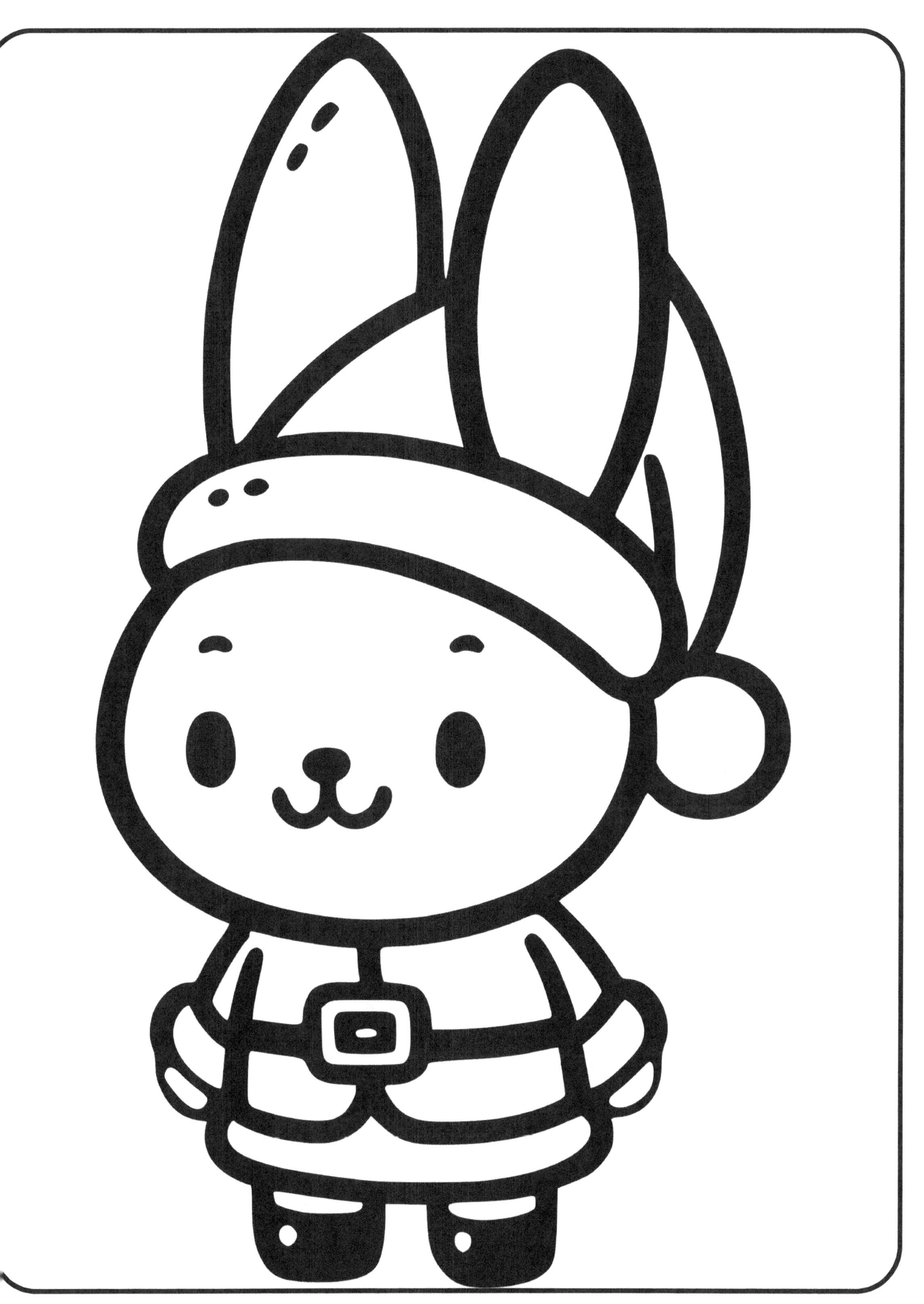

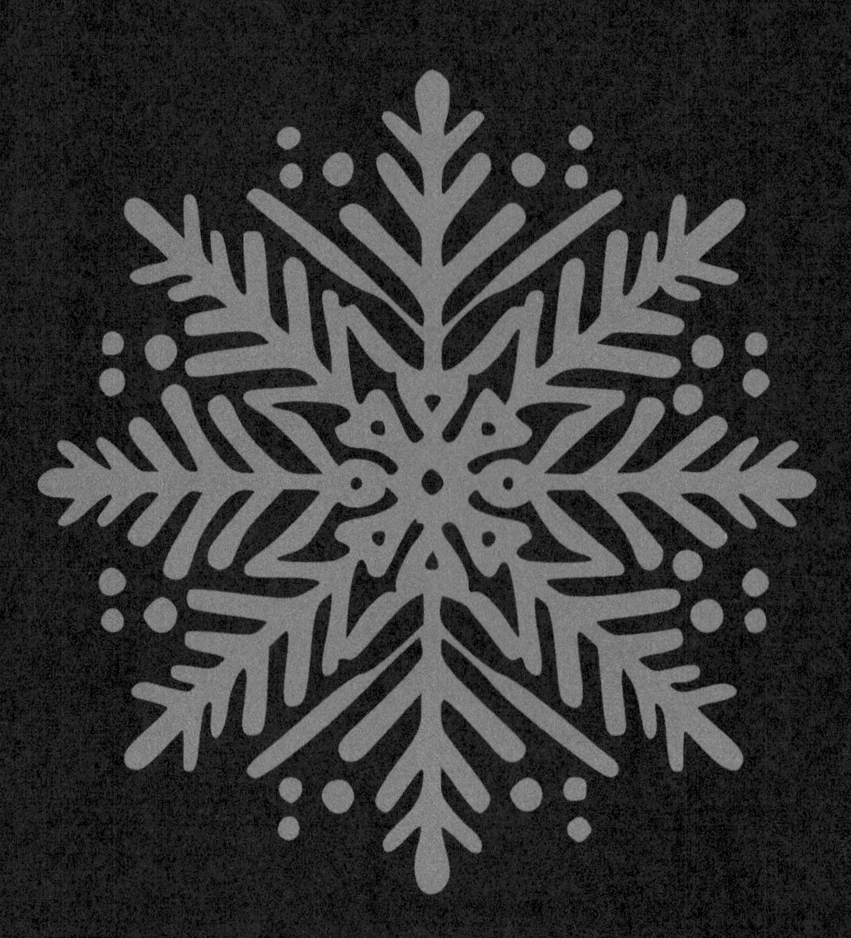

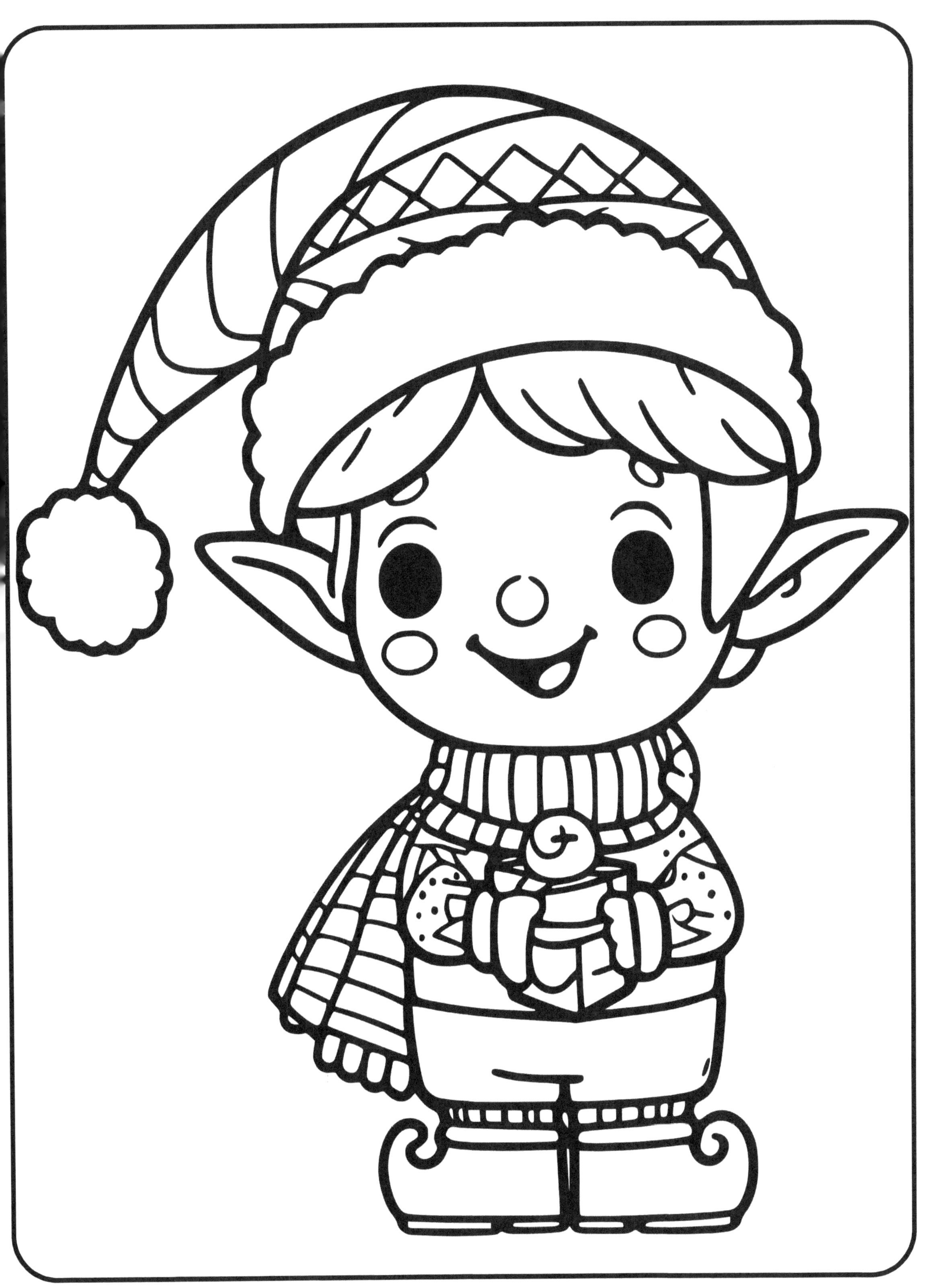

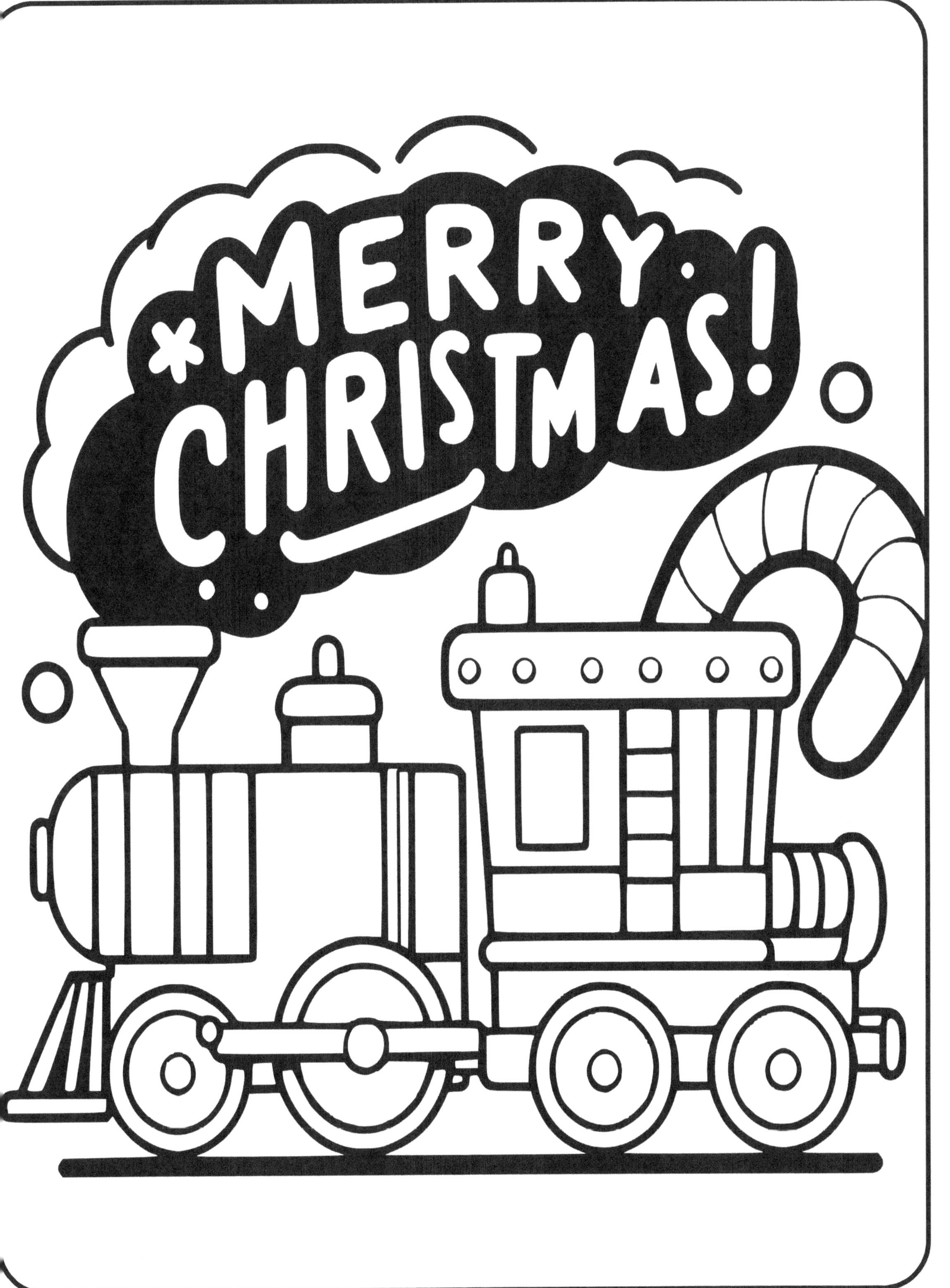

MERRY CHRISTMAS!

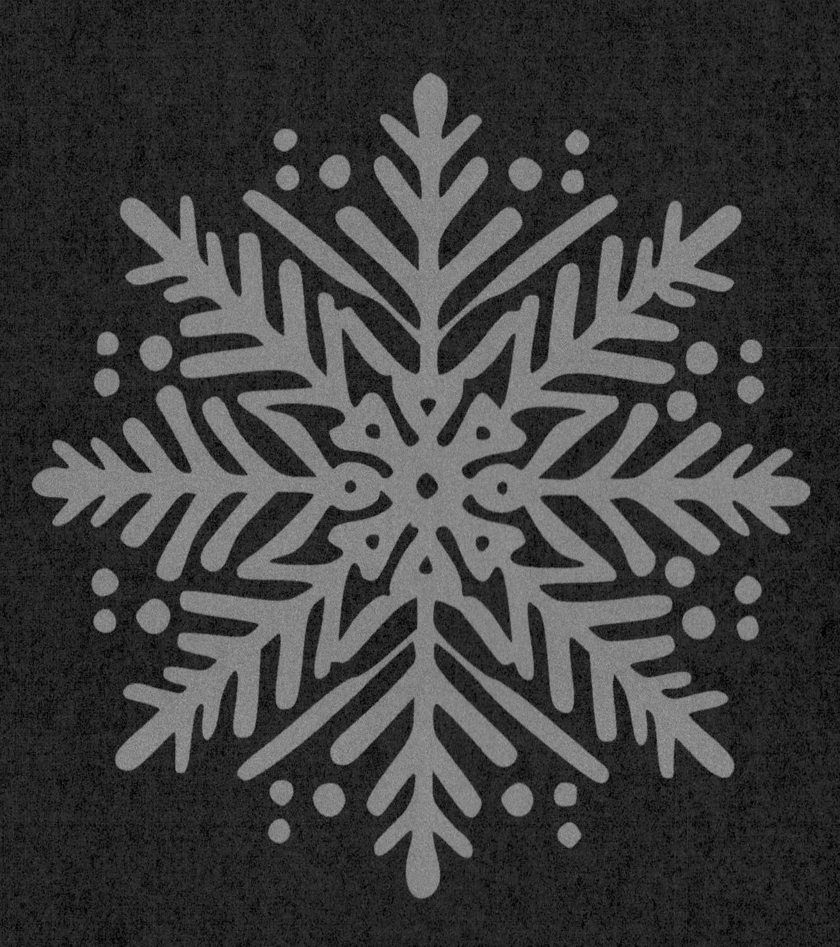

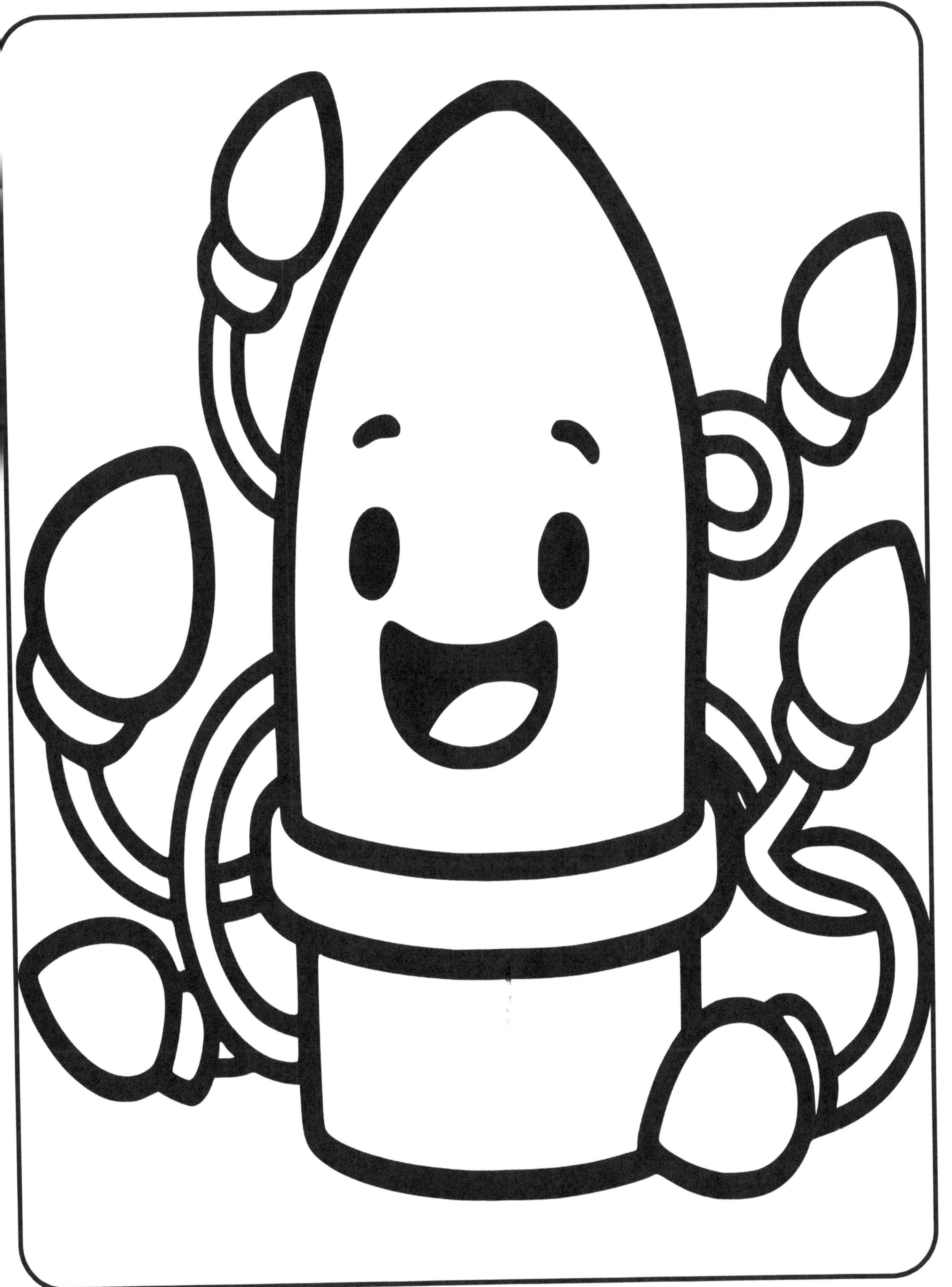

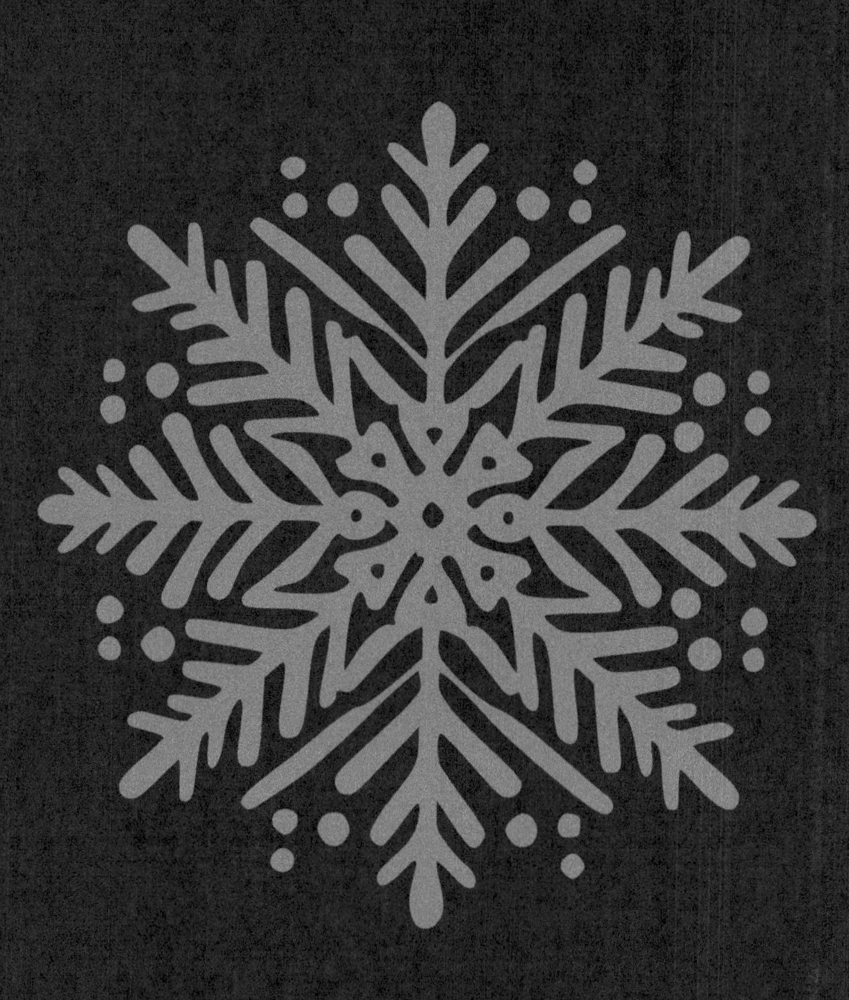

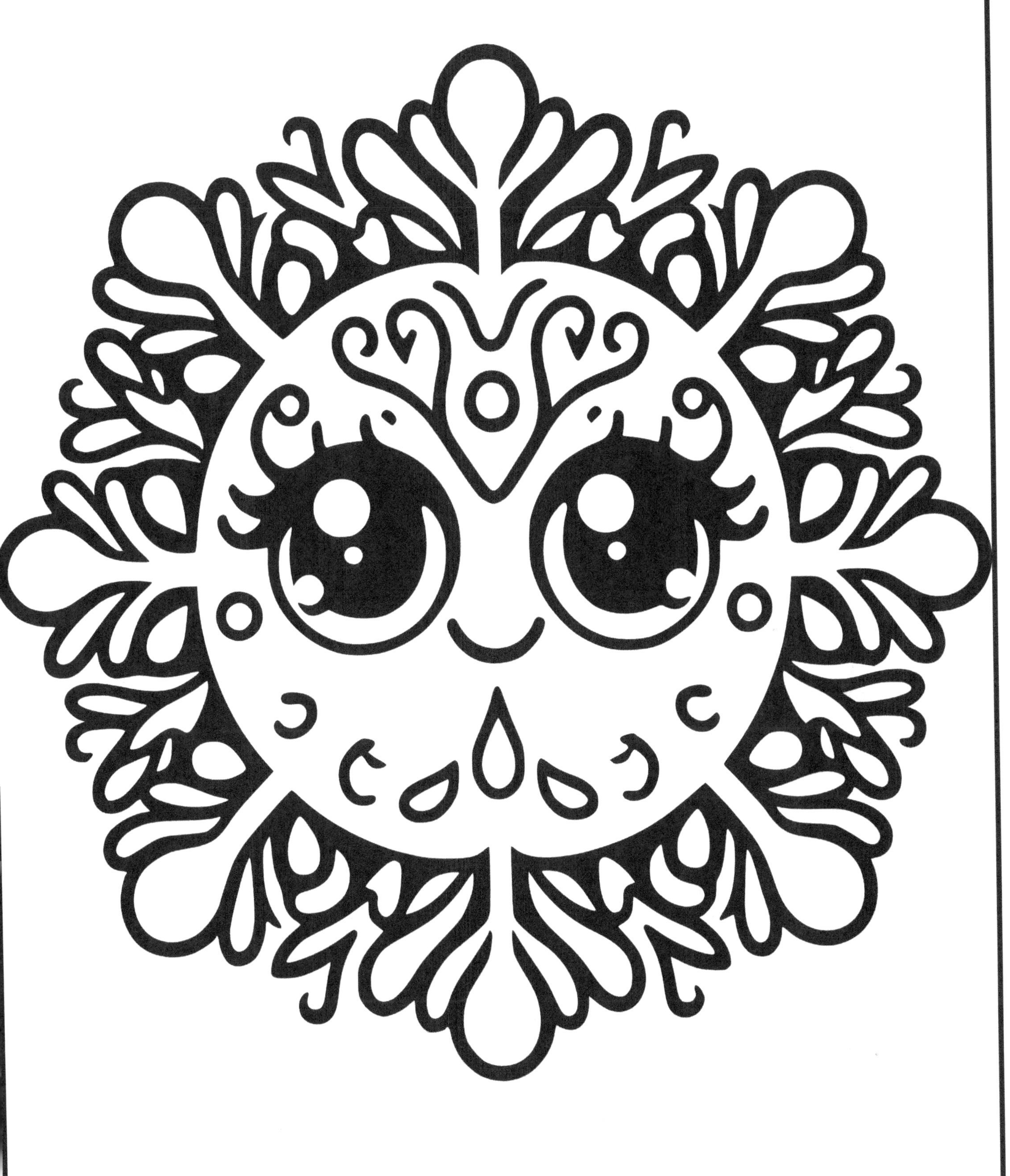

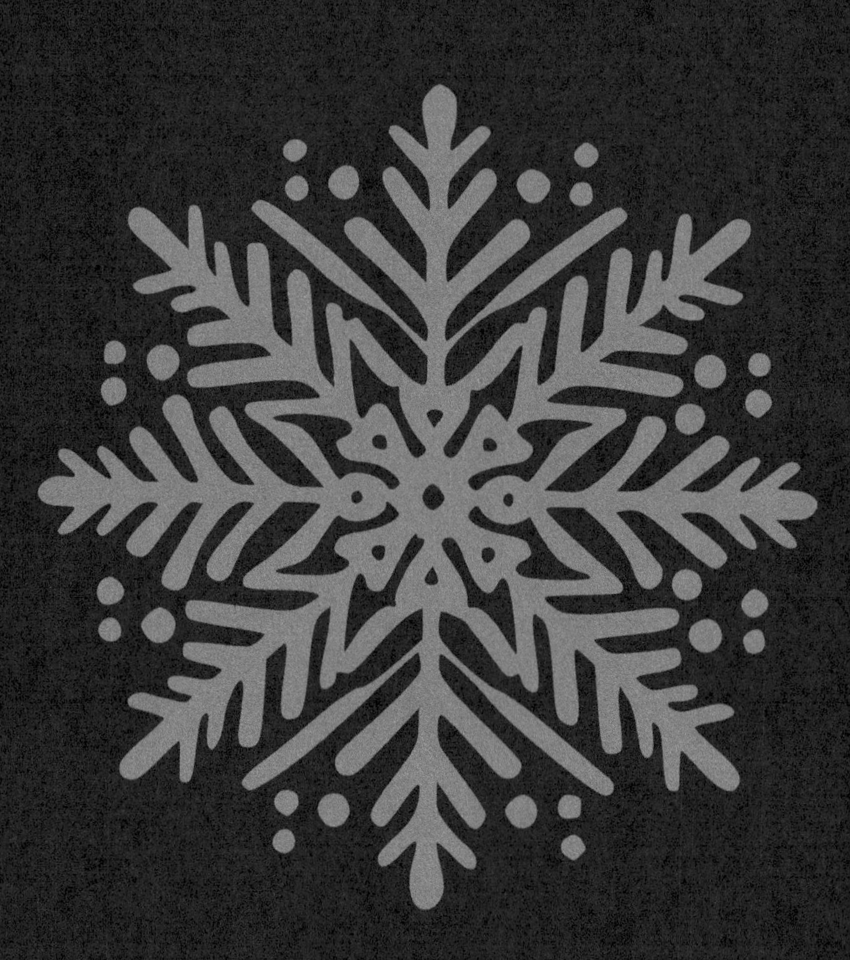

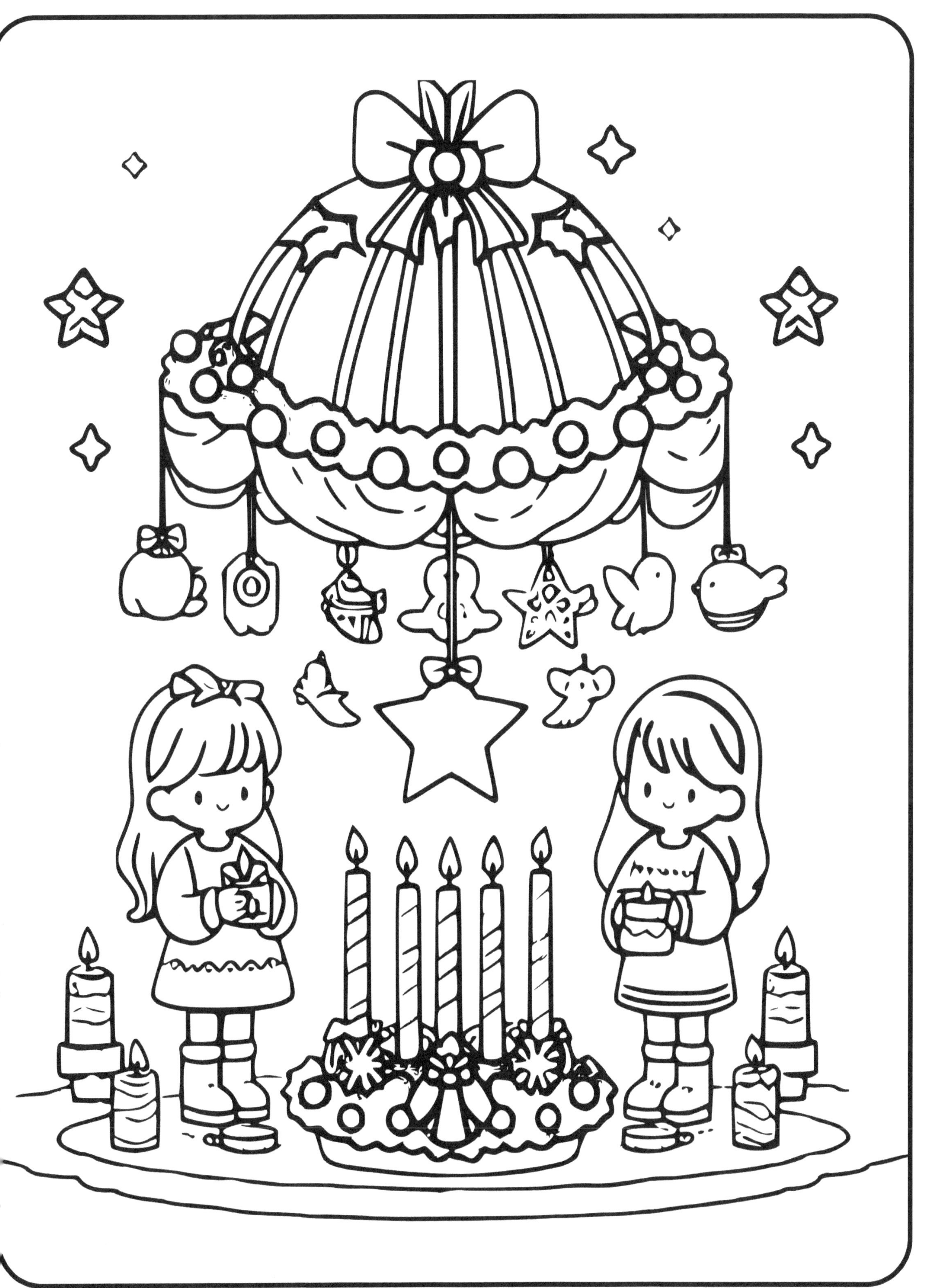

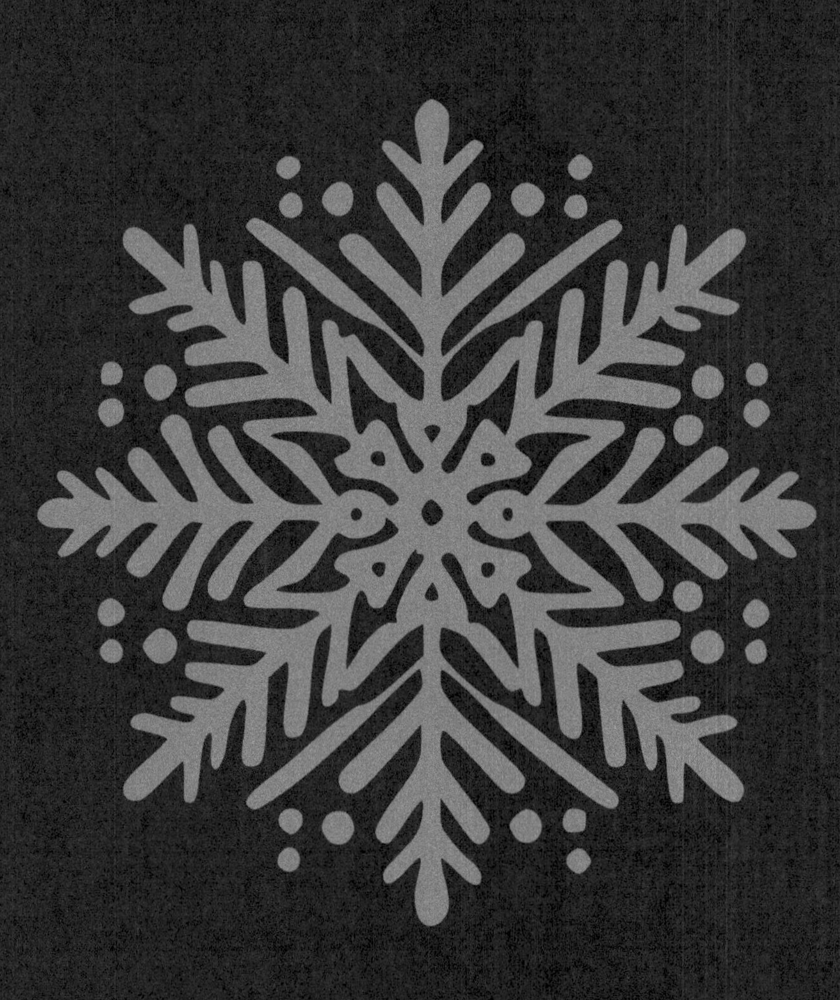

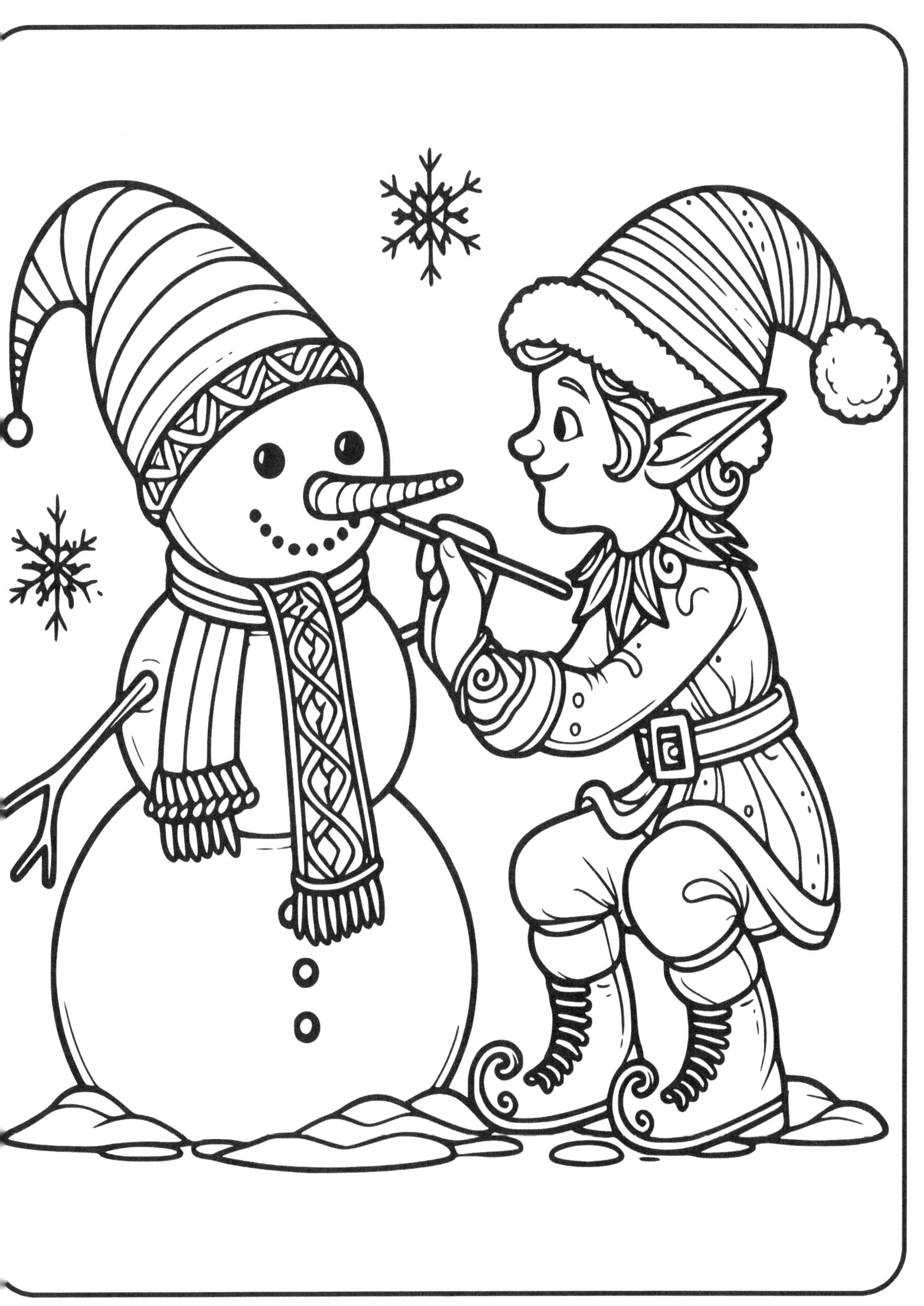

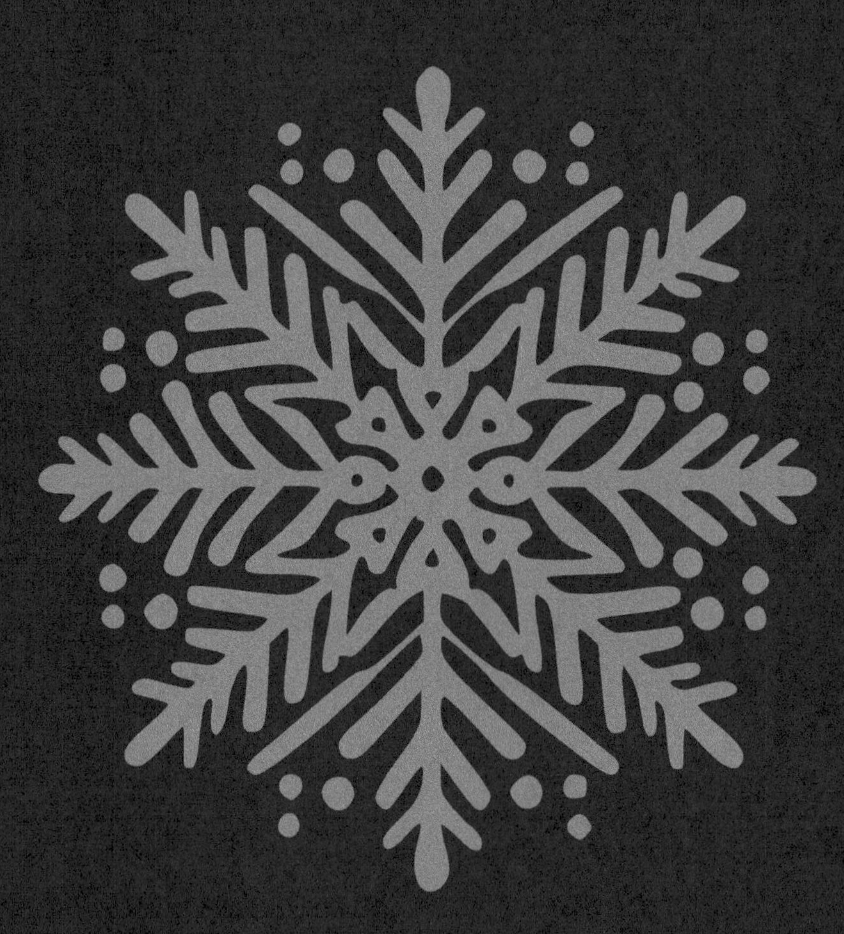

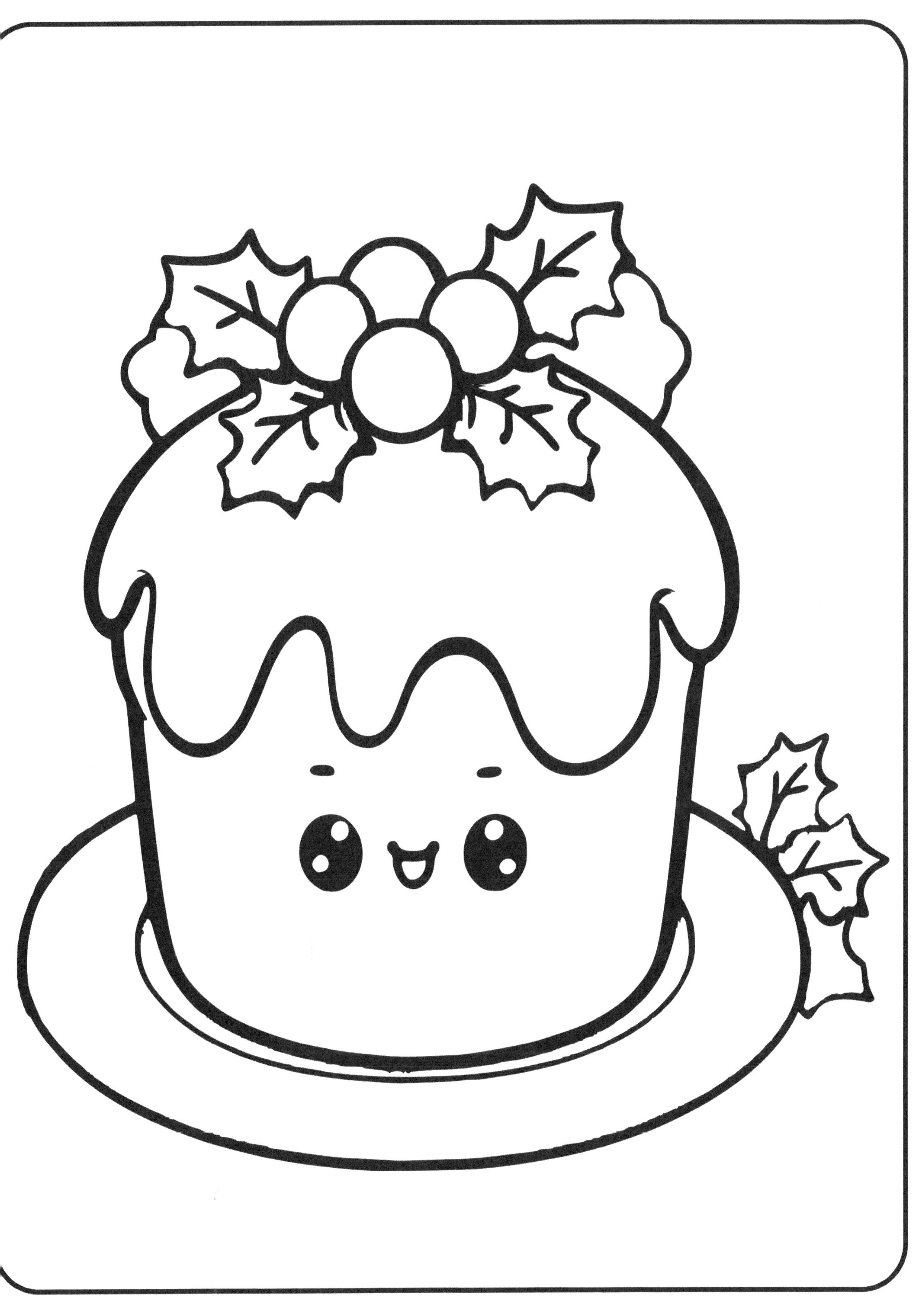

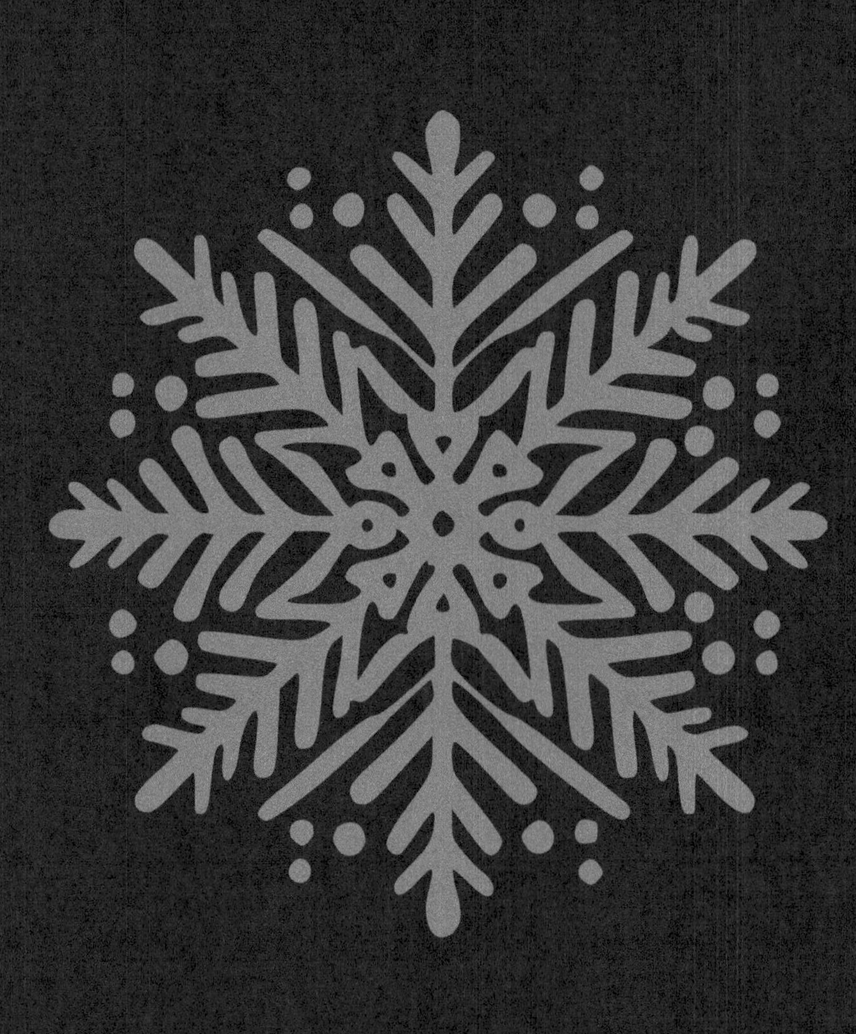

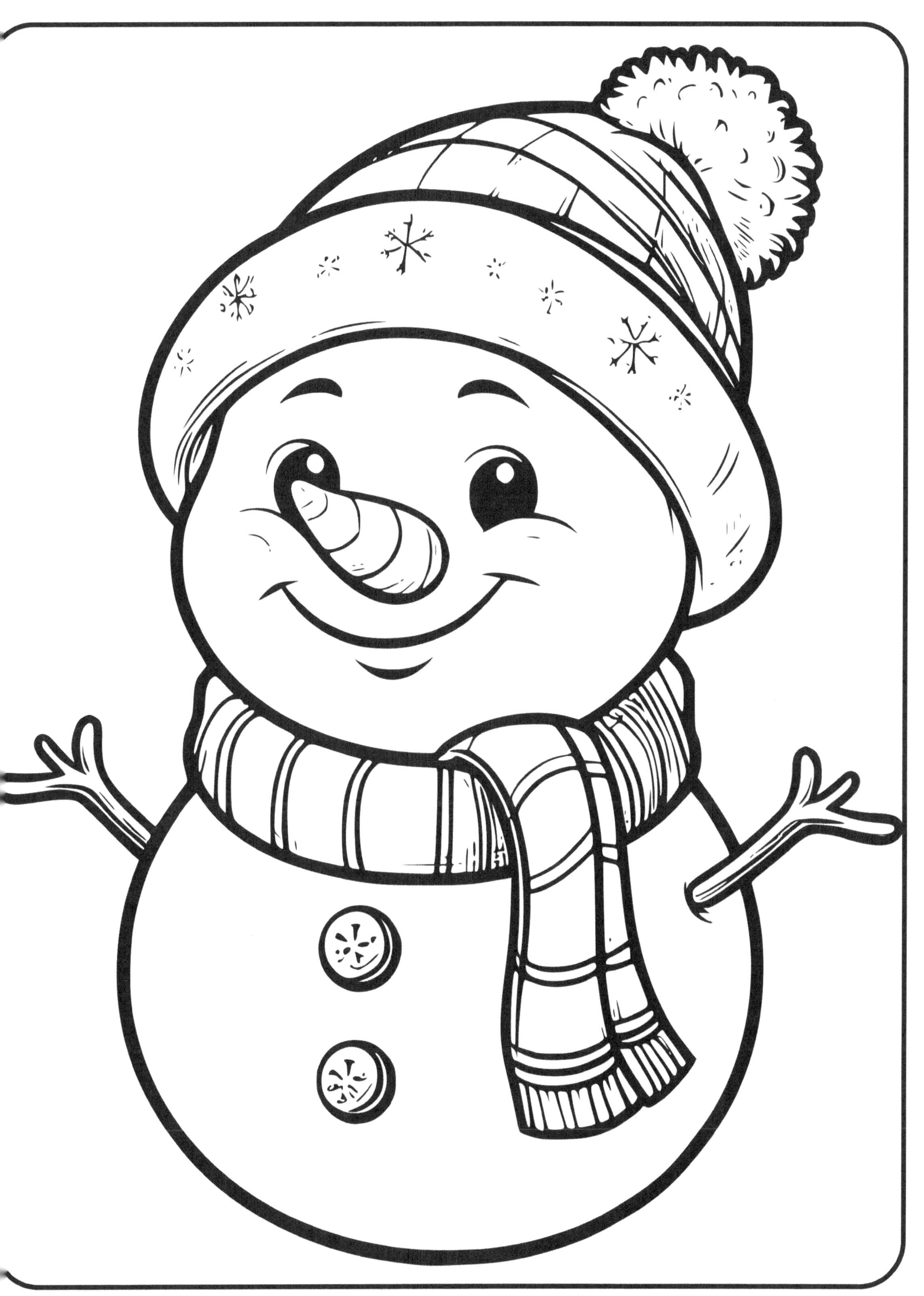

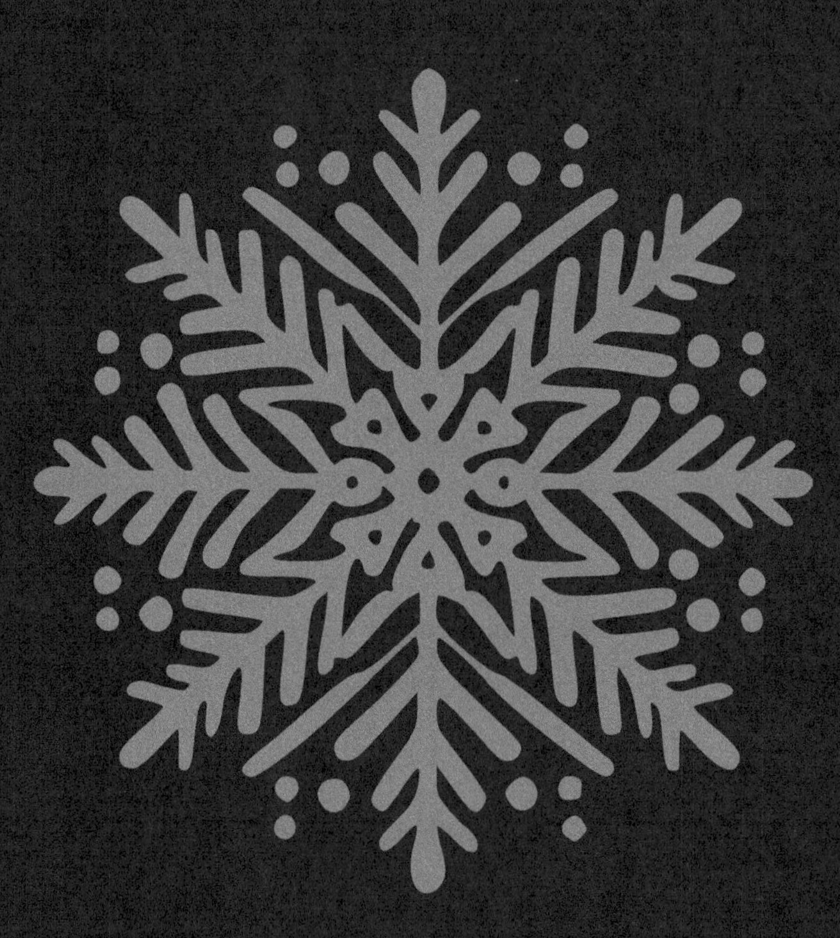

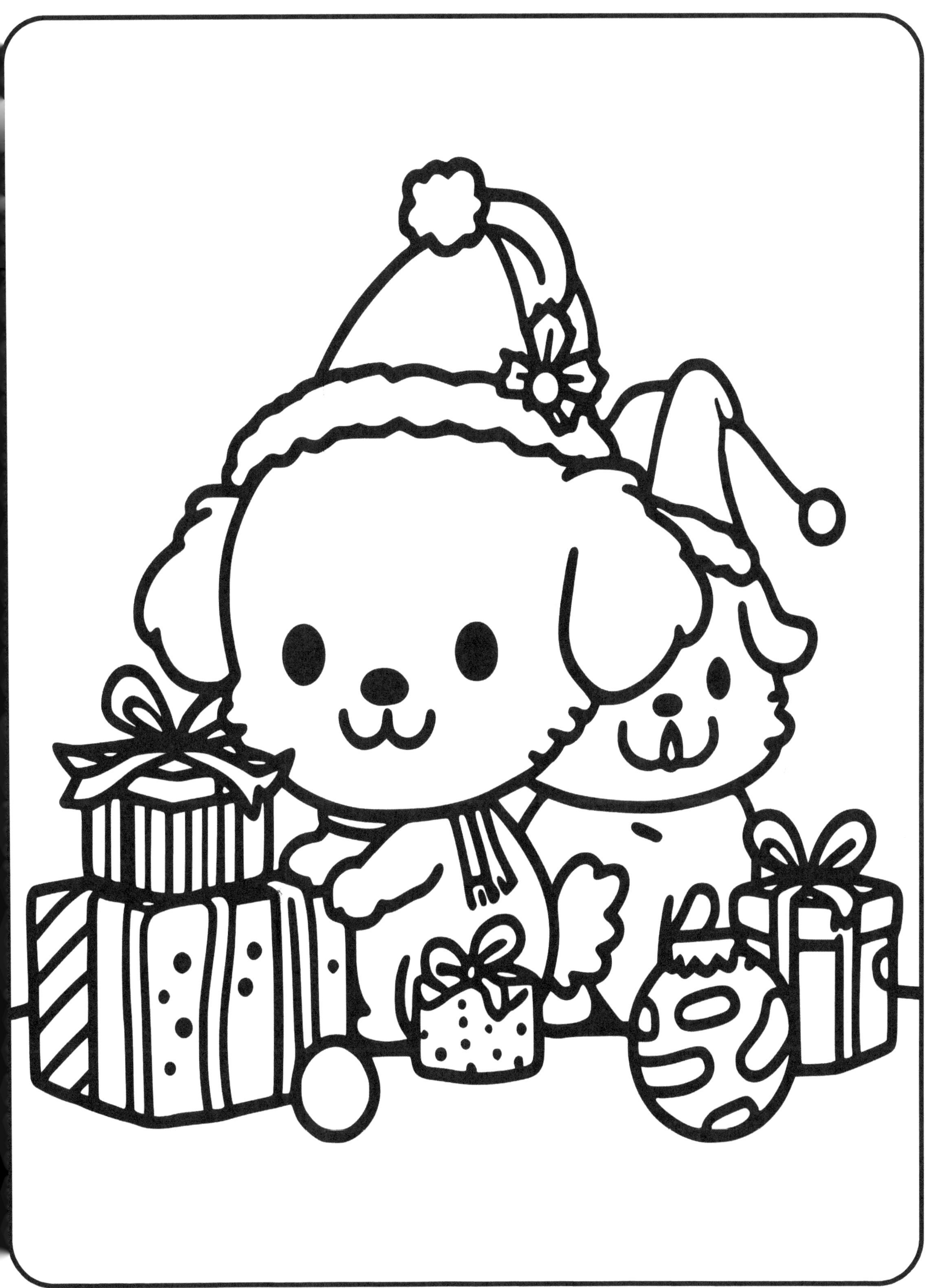

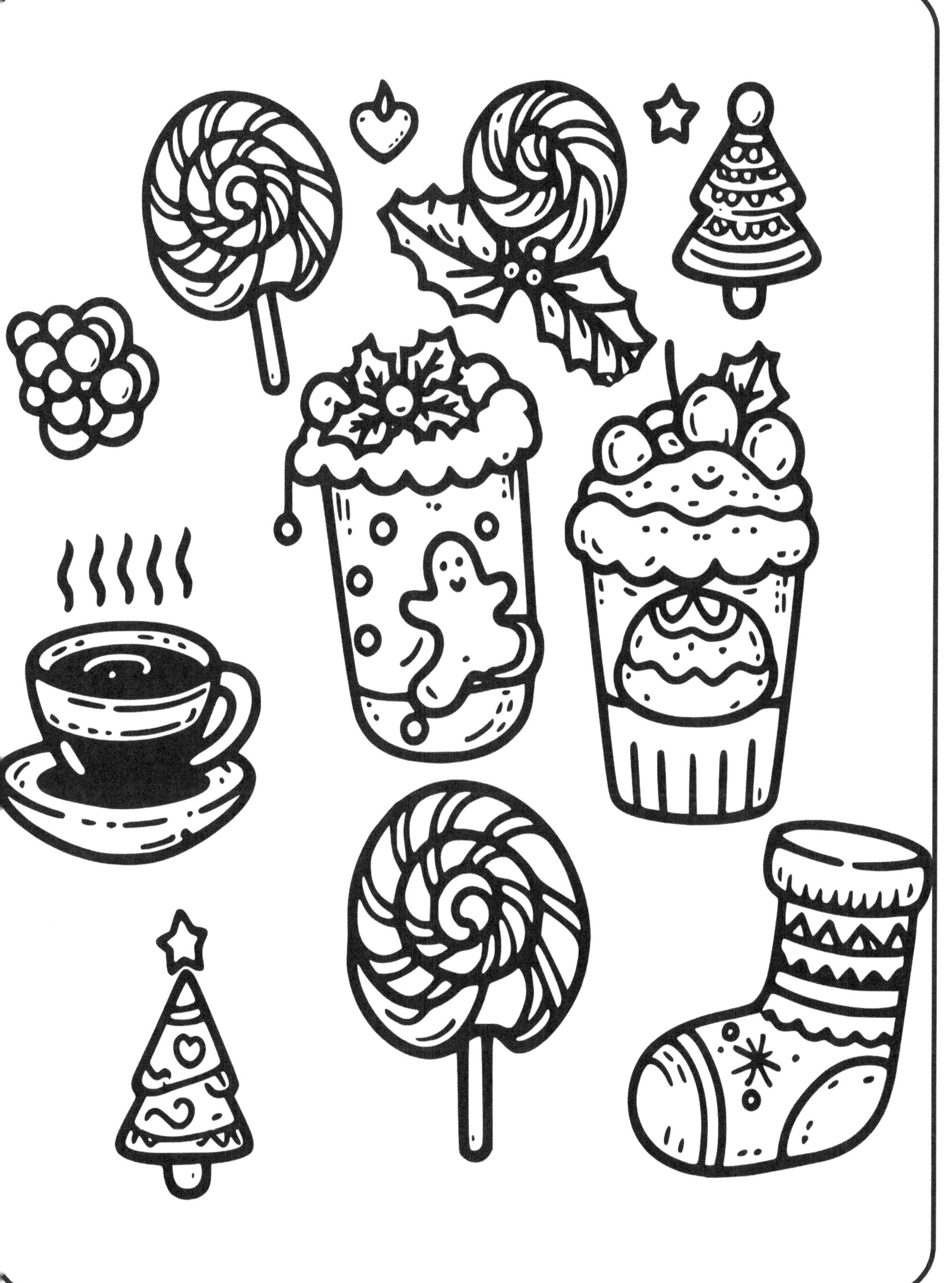

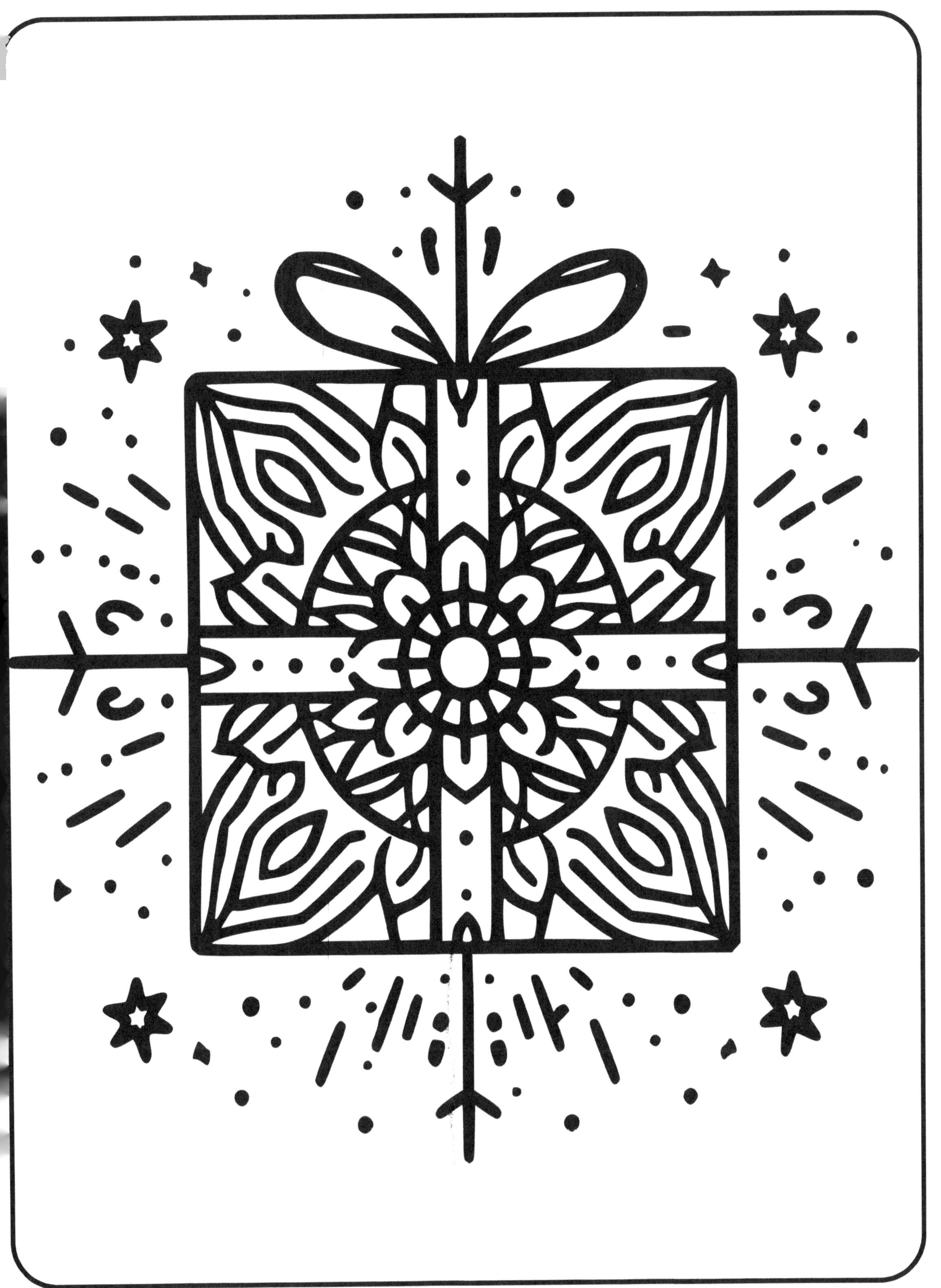

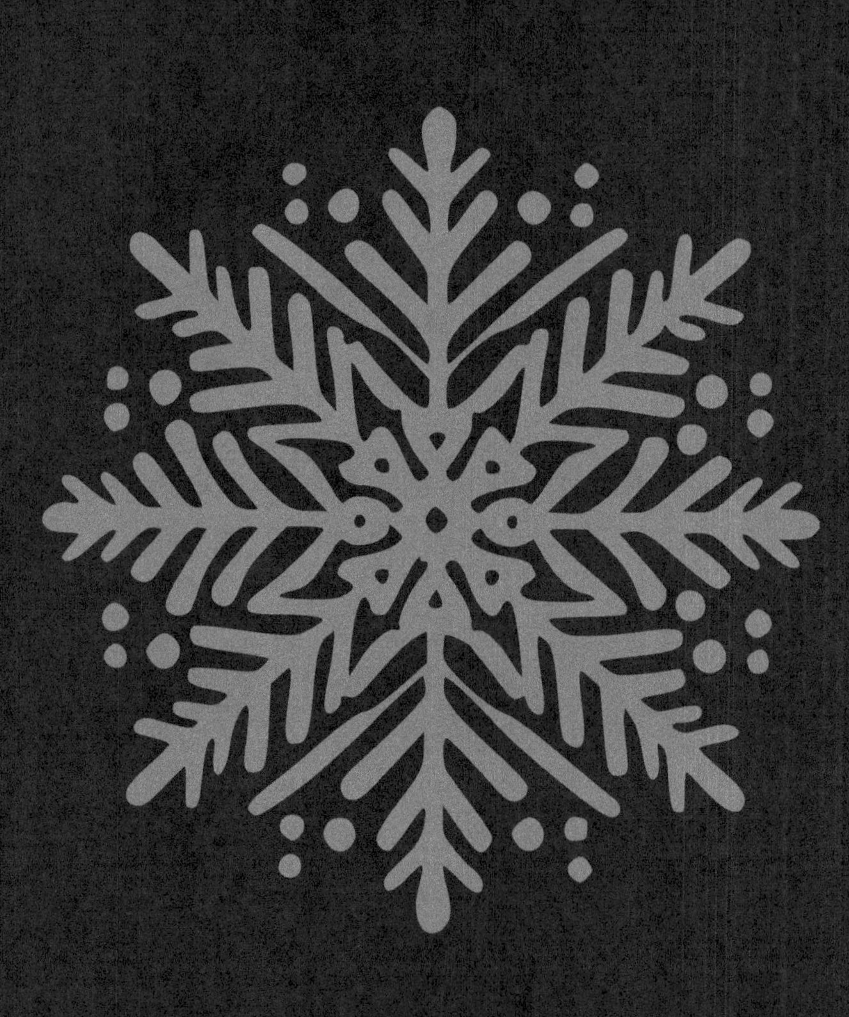

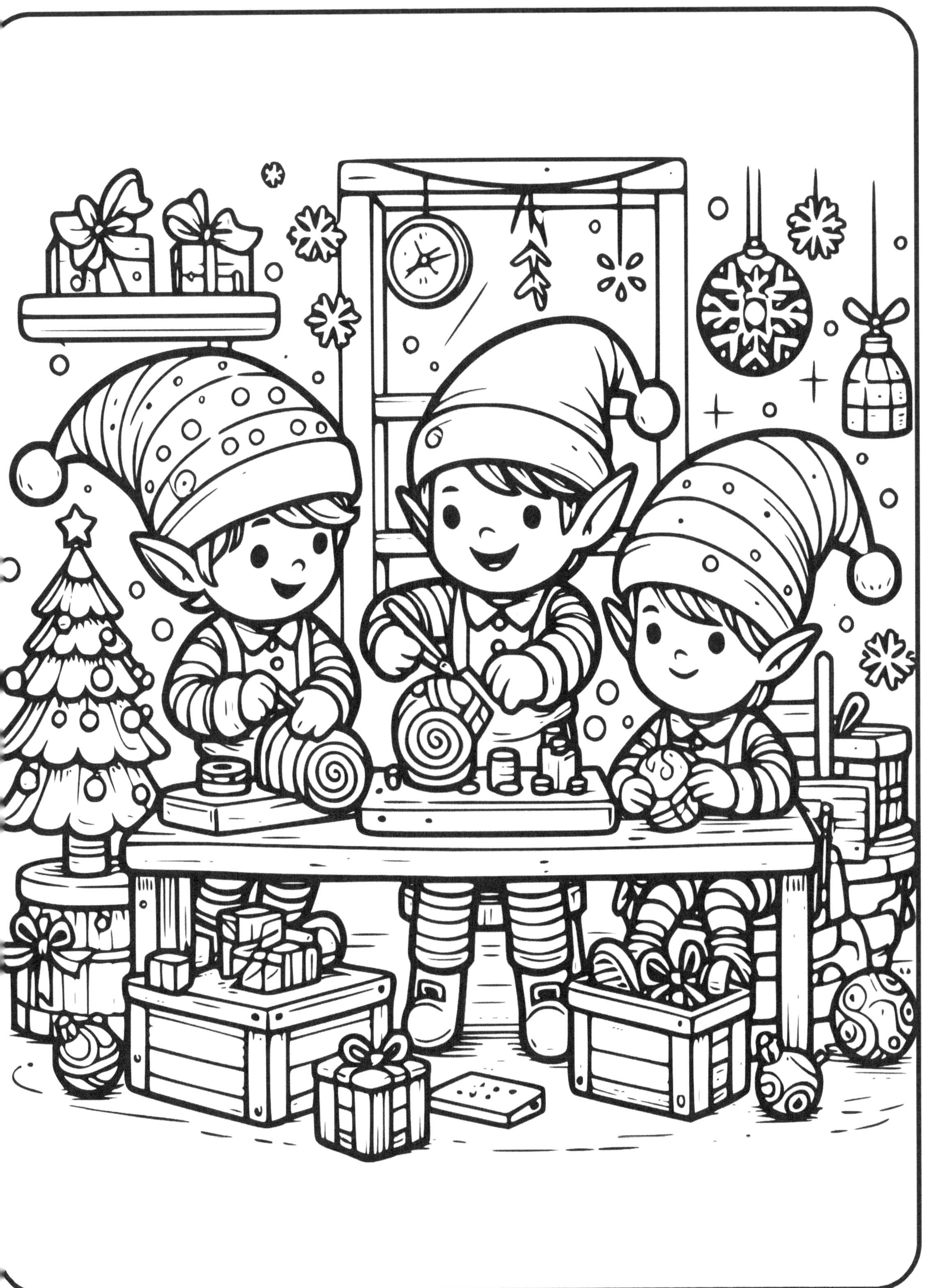

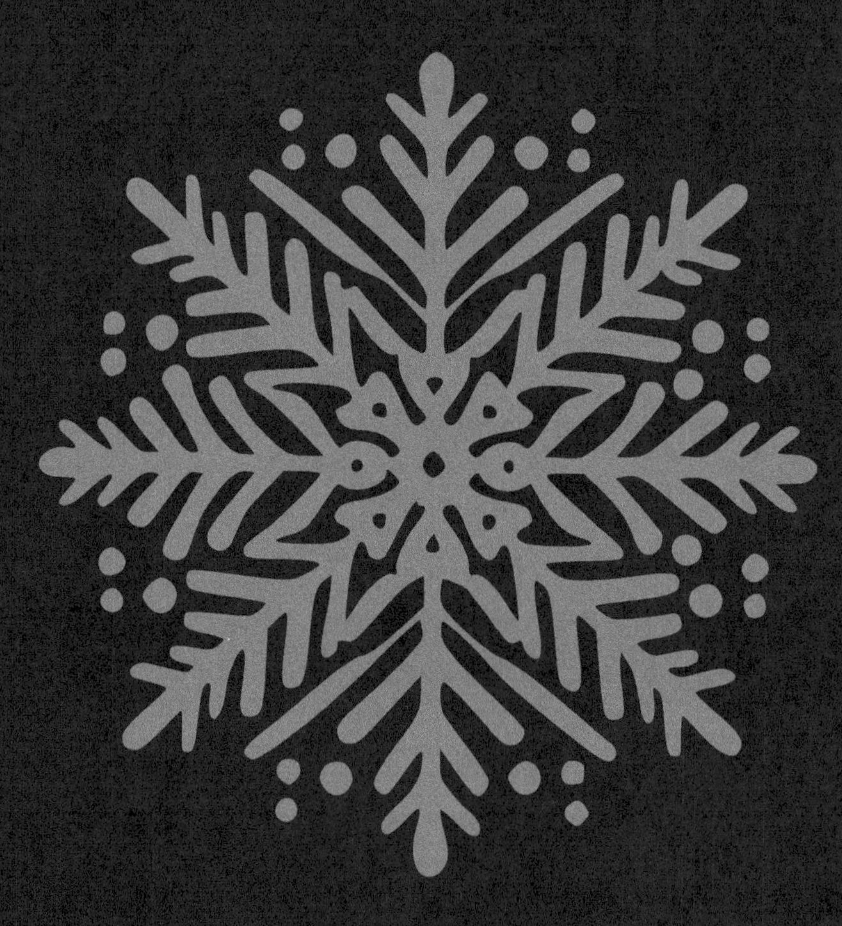

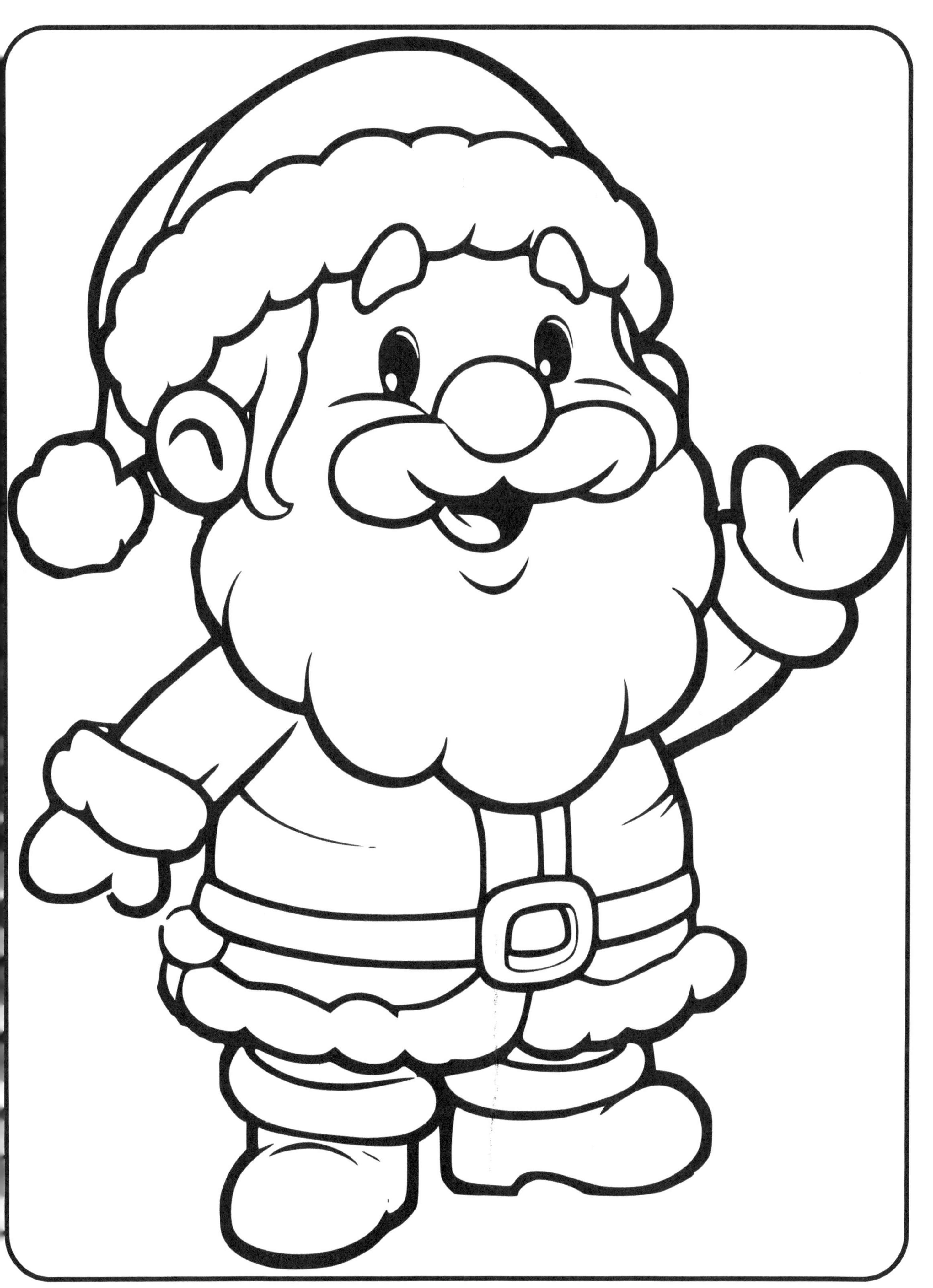

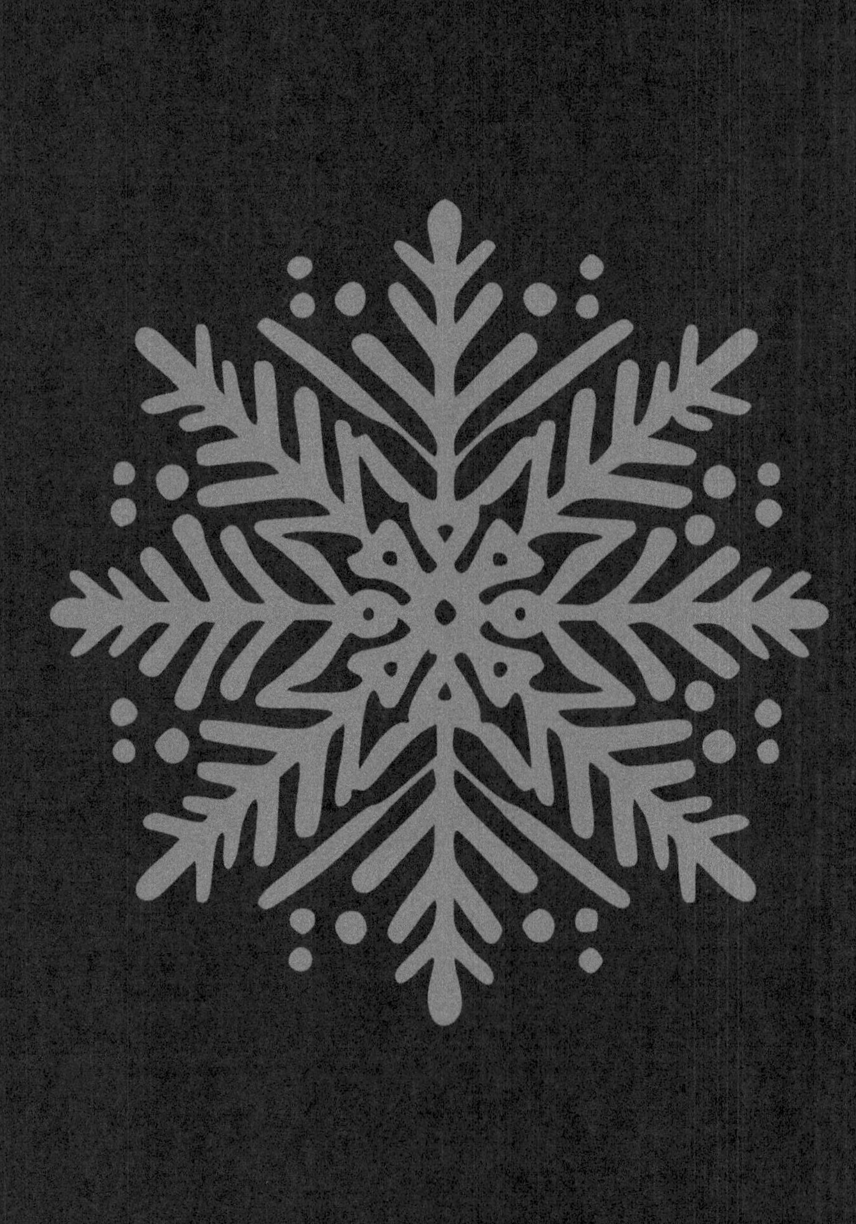

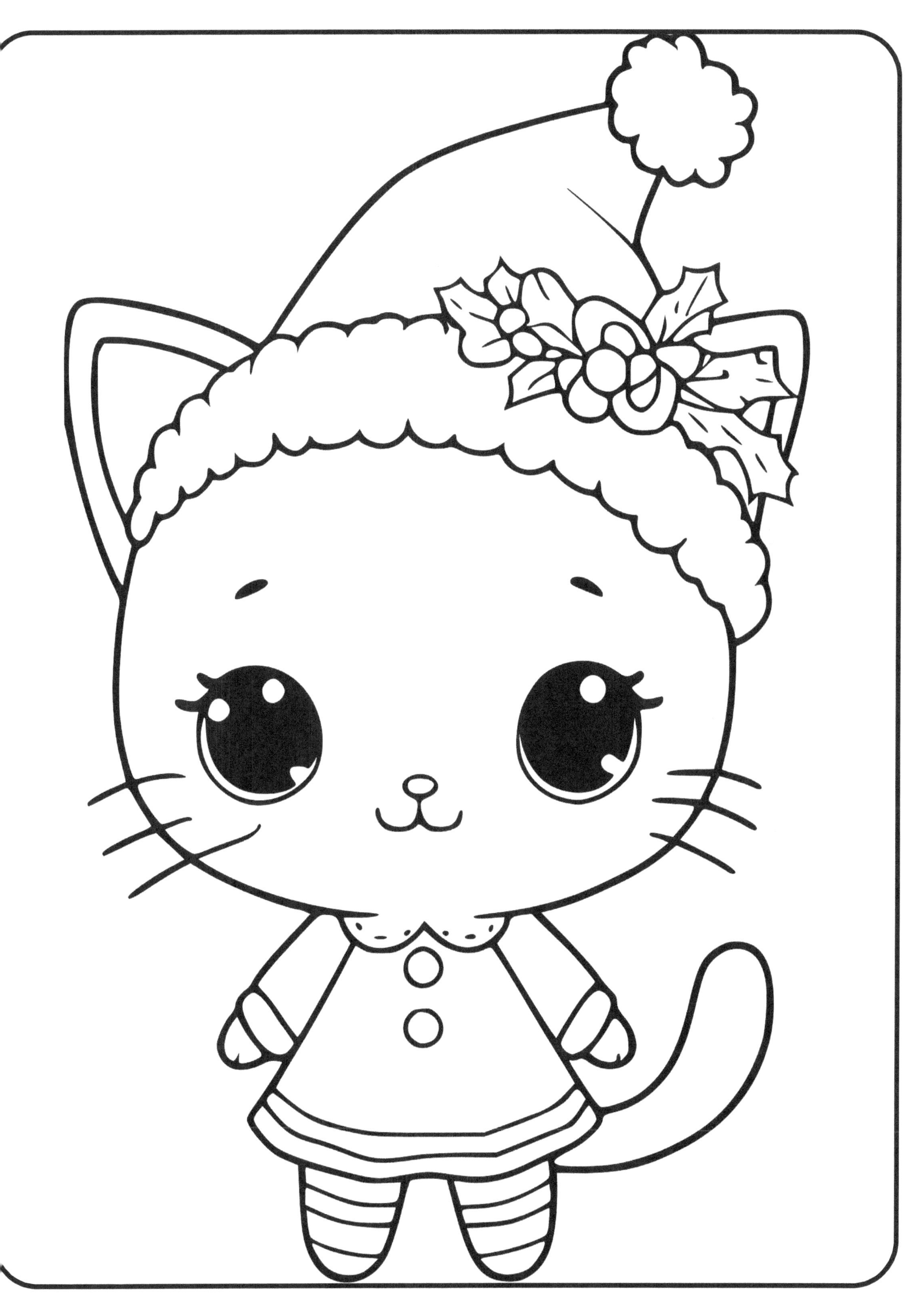

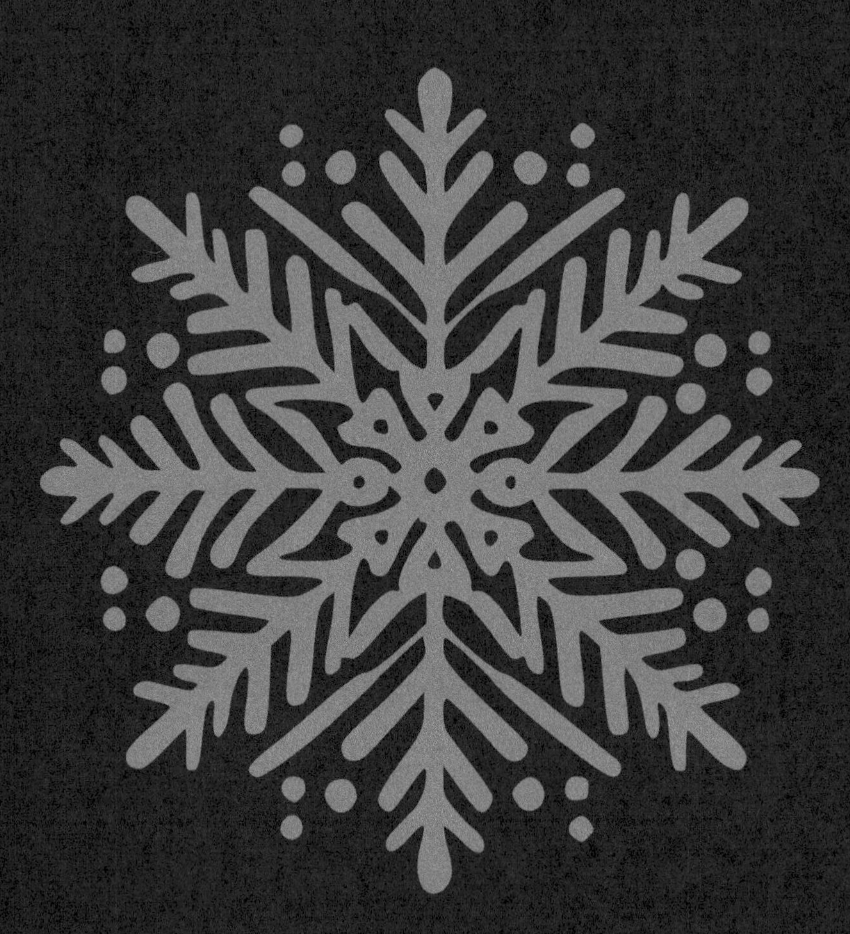

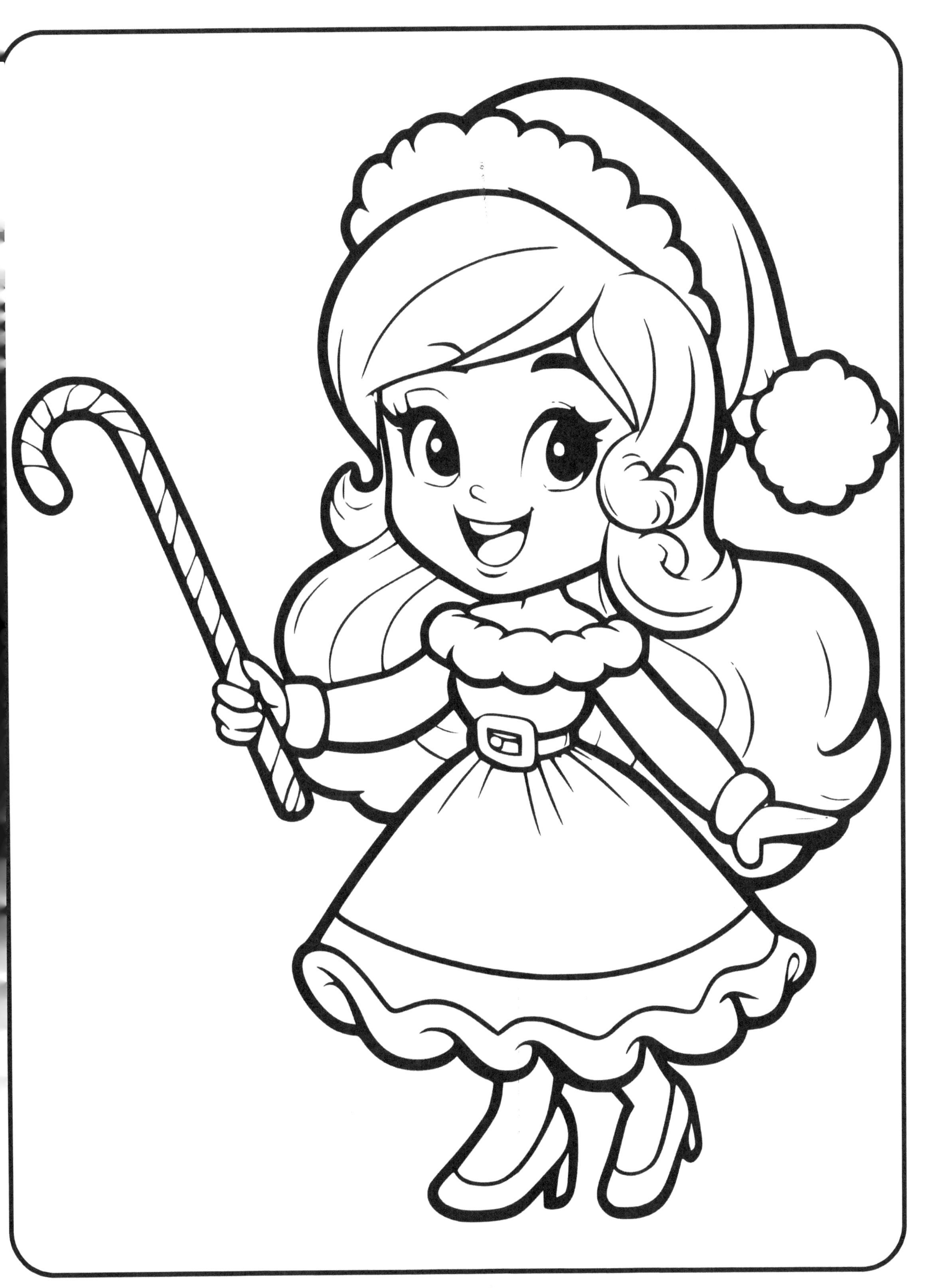

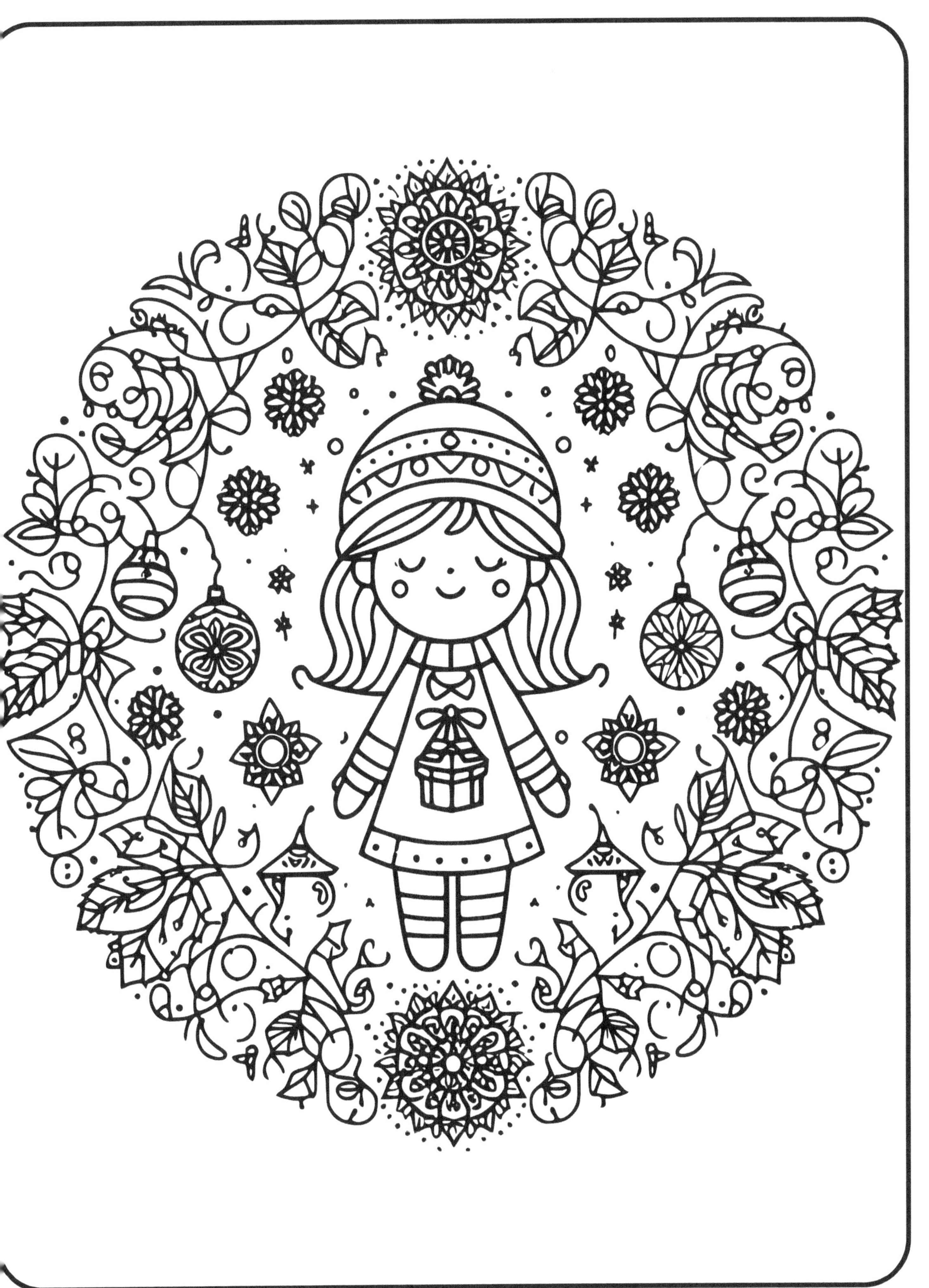

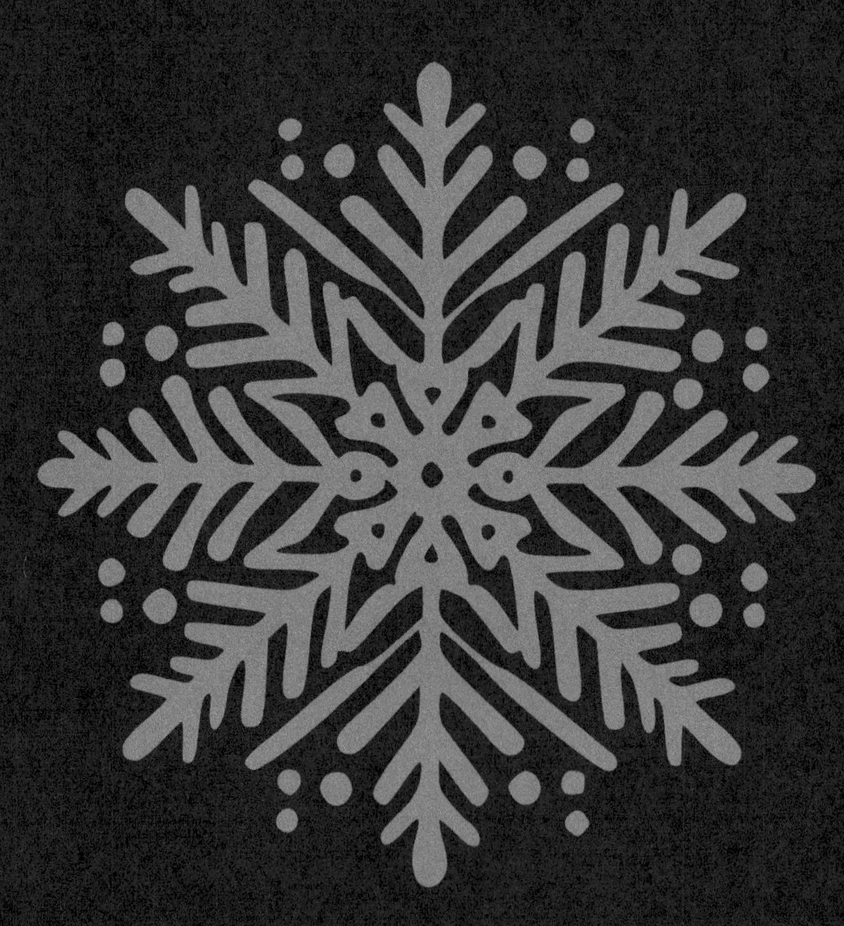

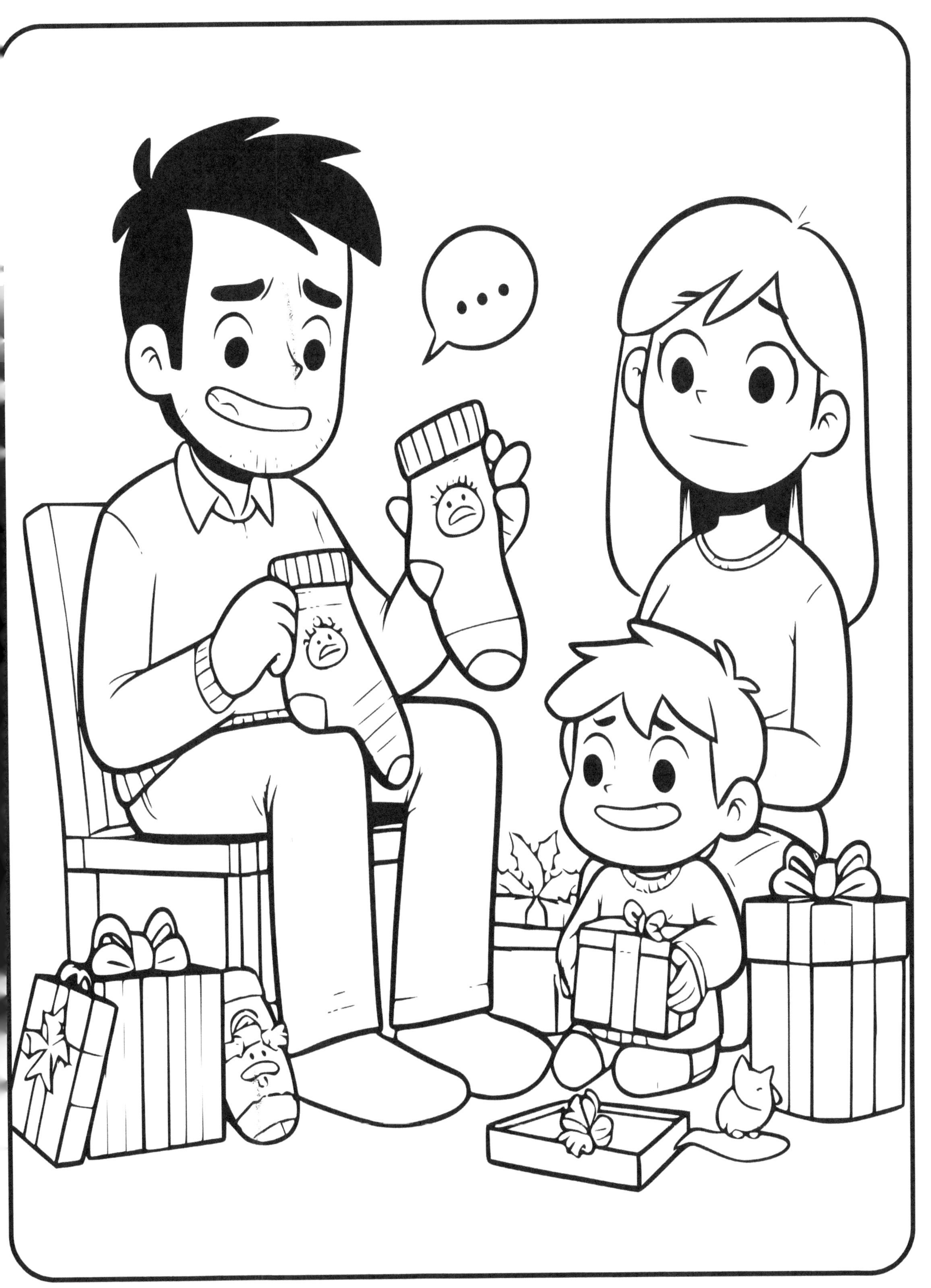

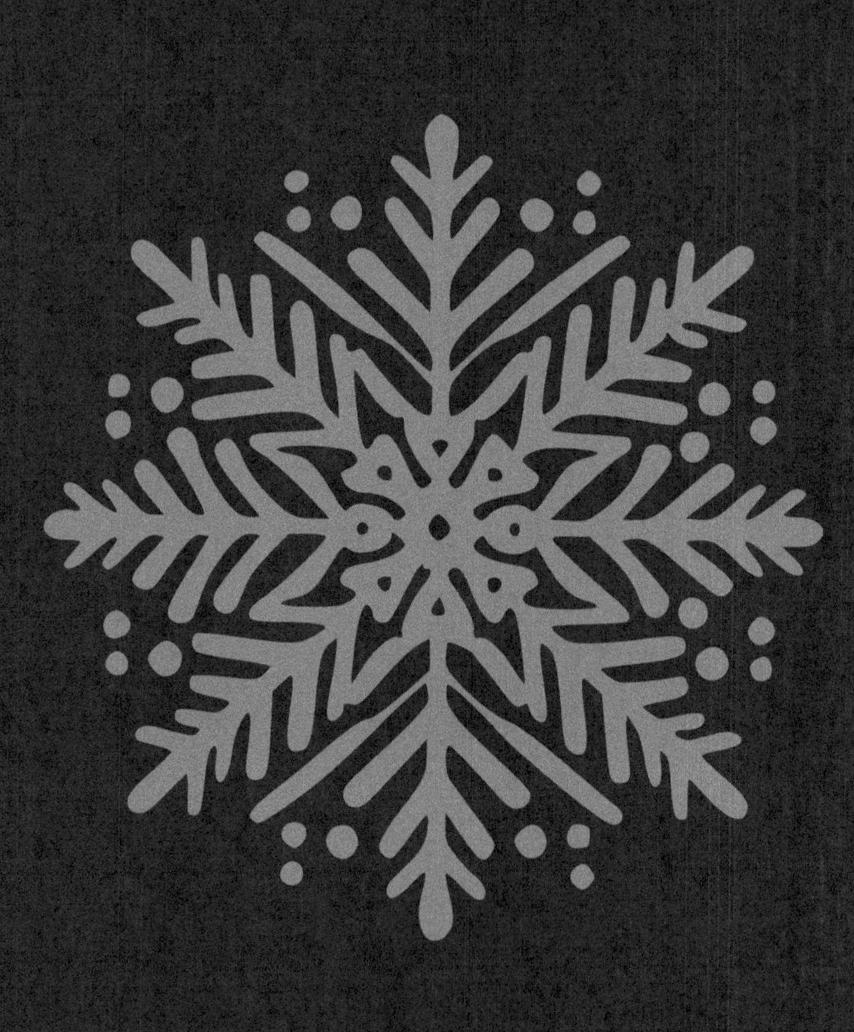

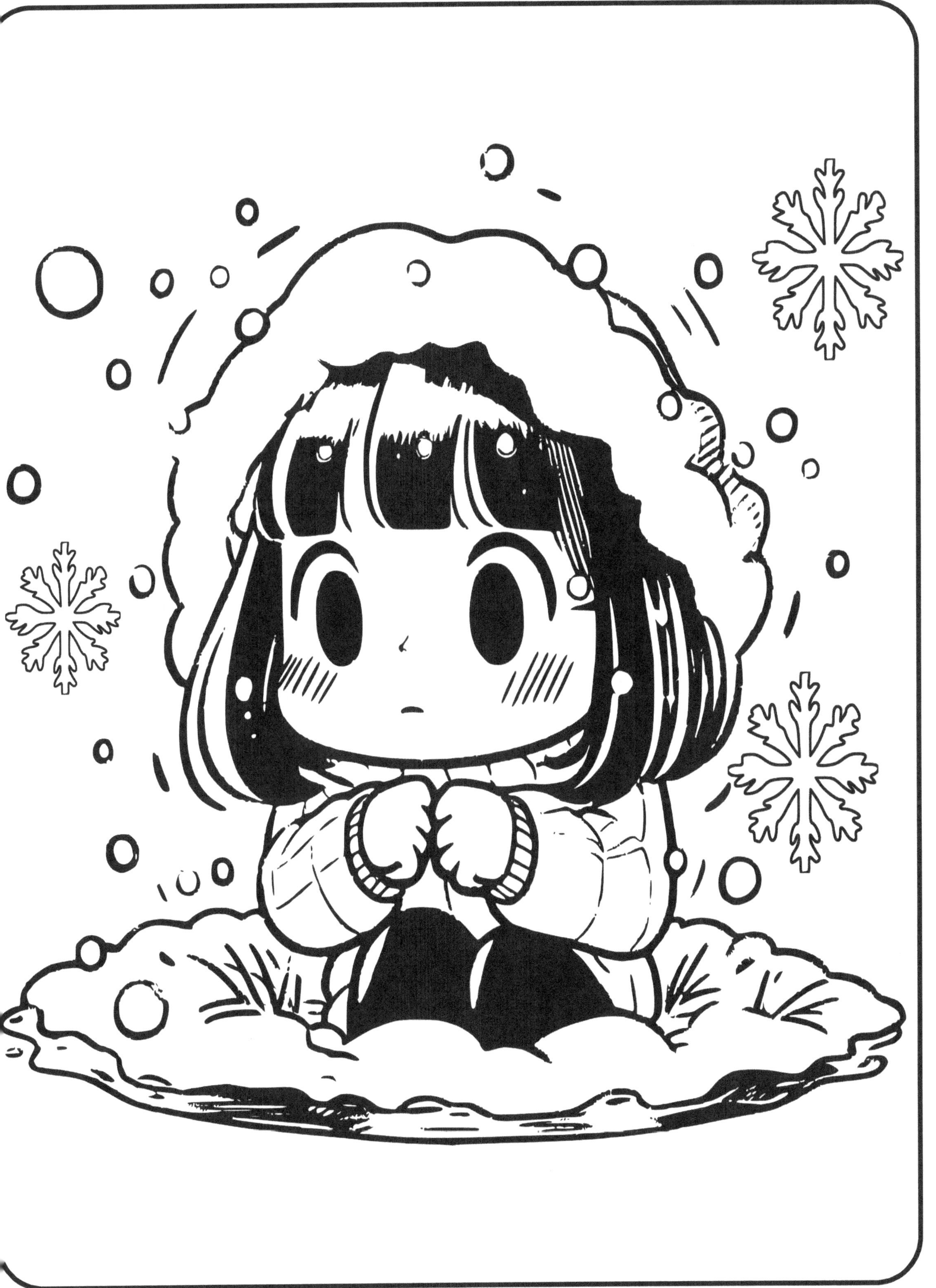

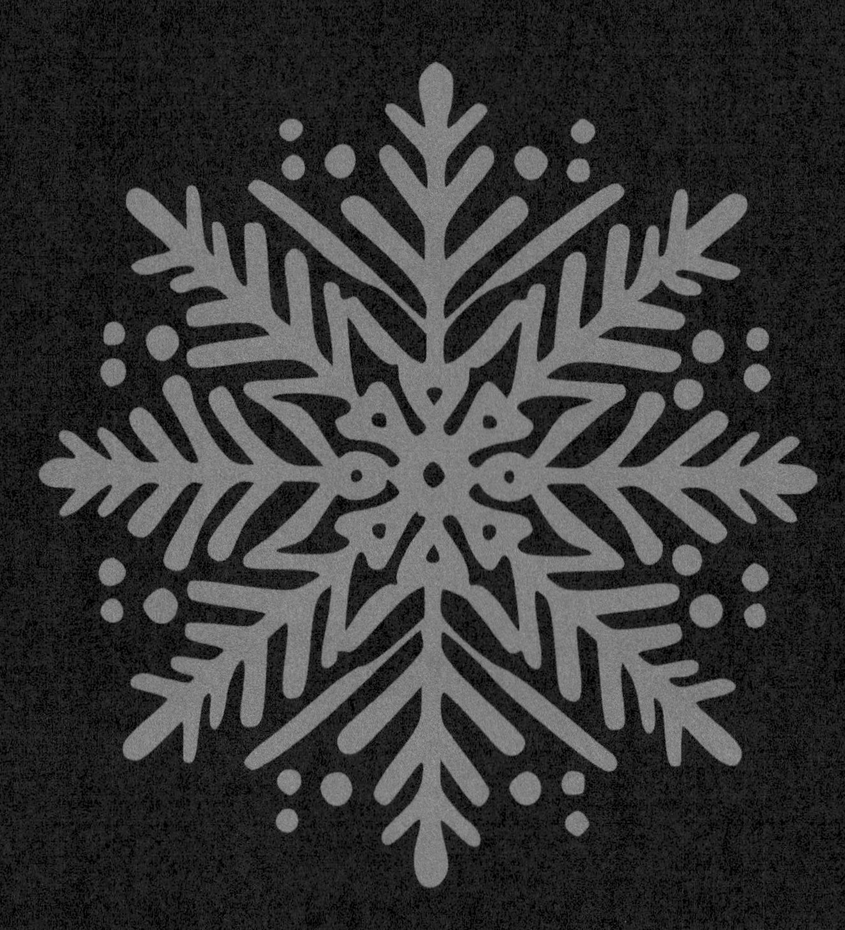

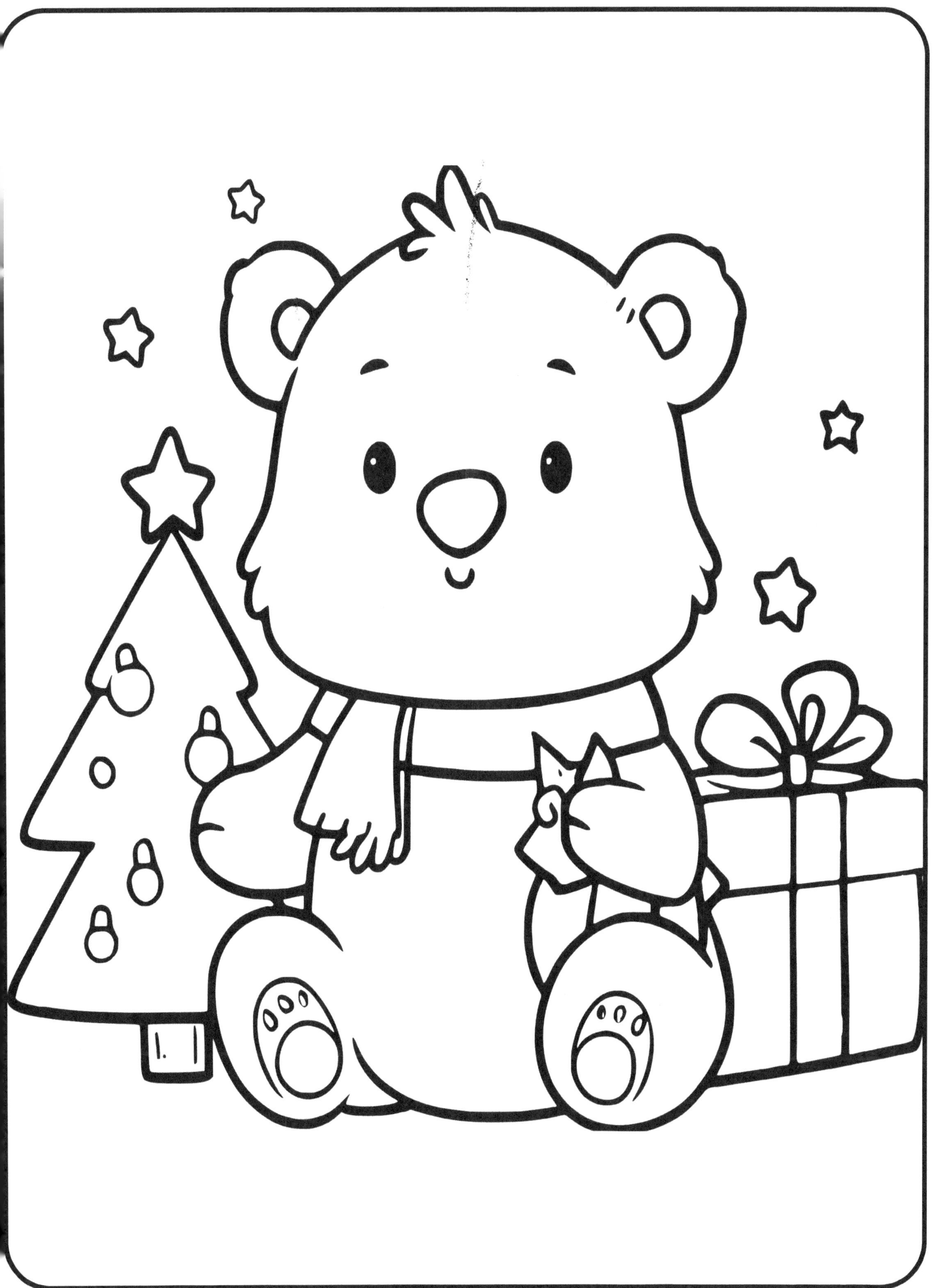

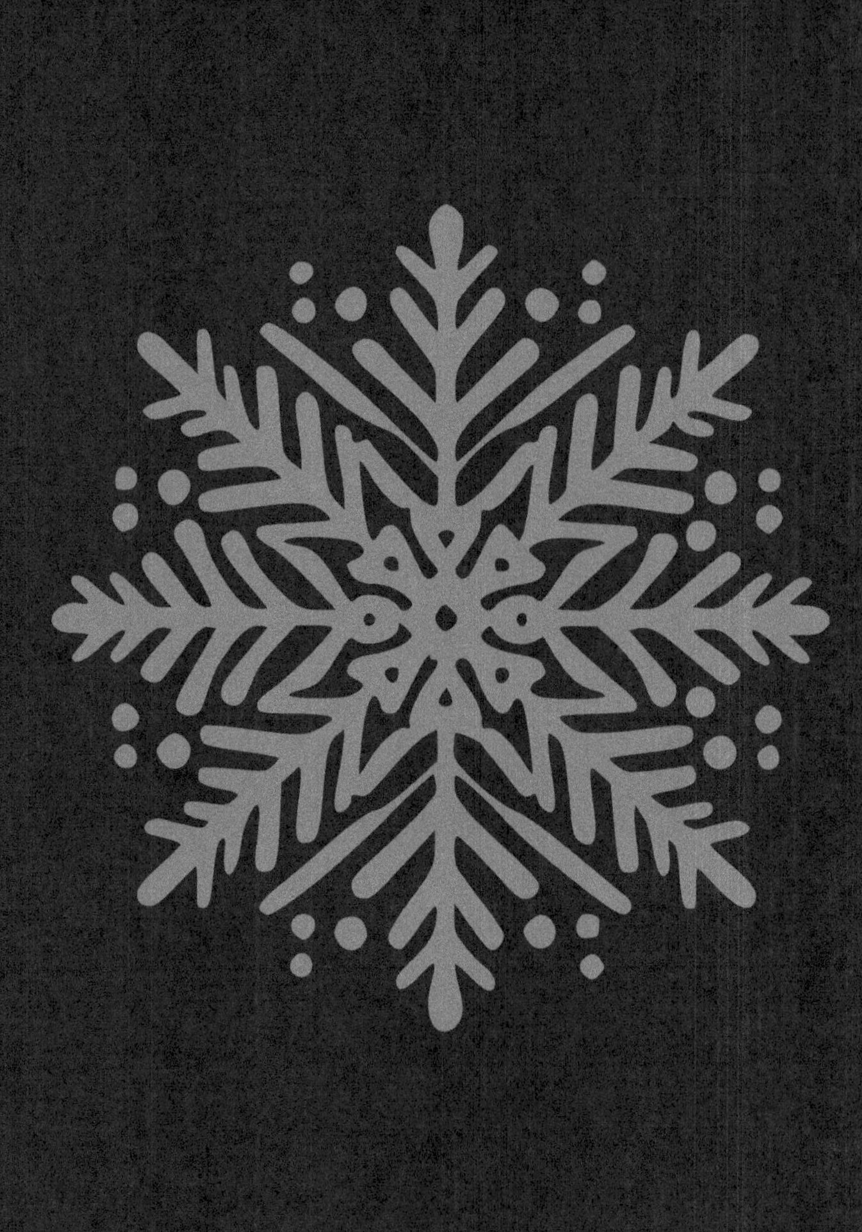

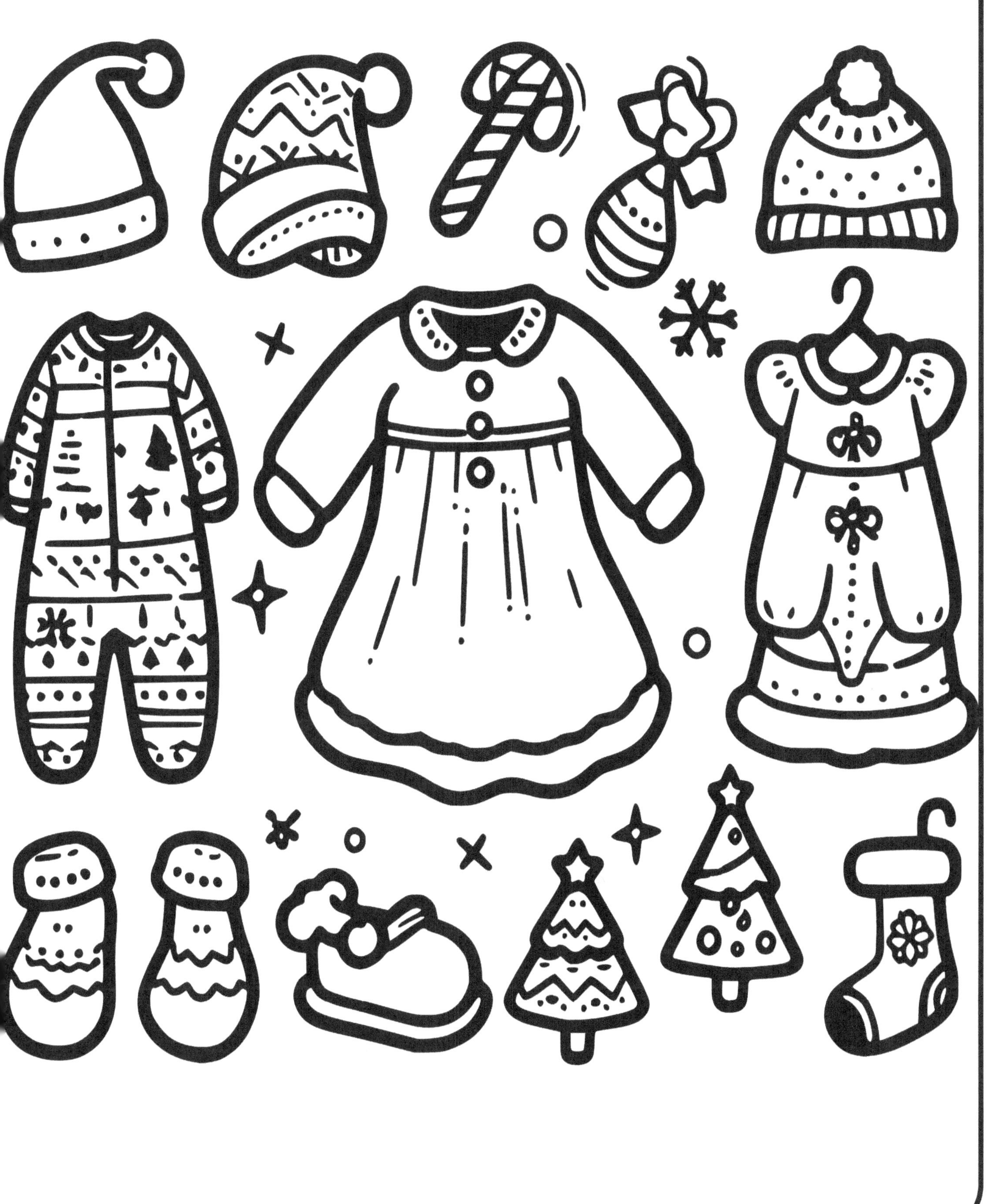

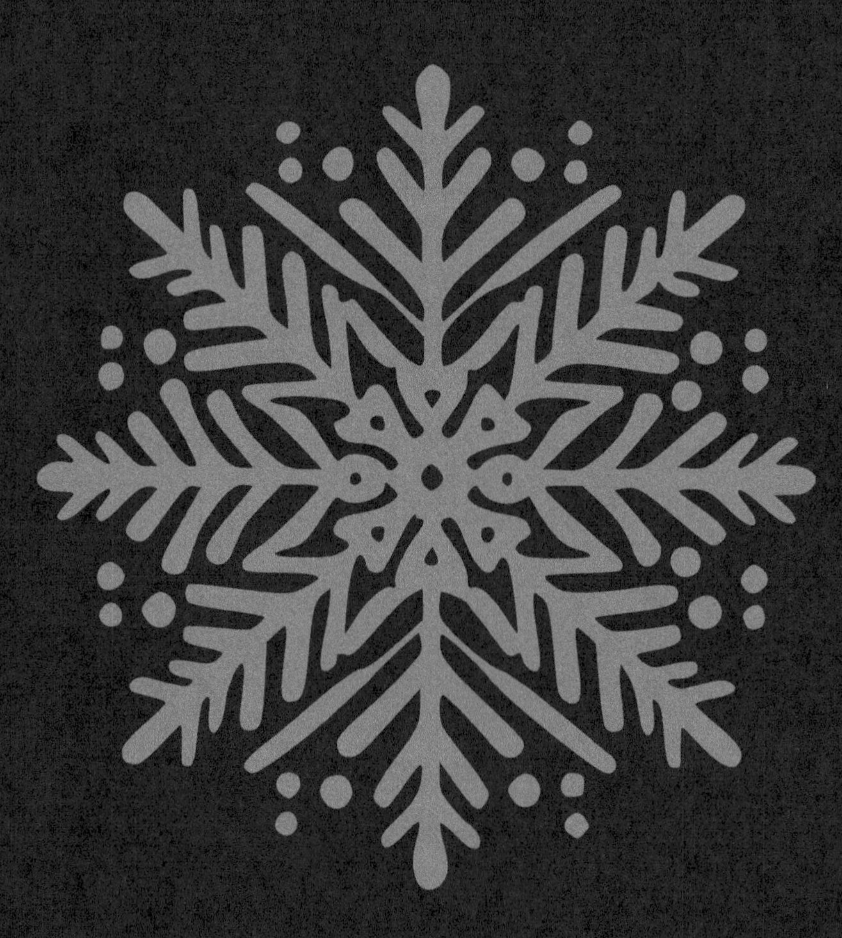

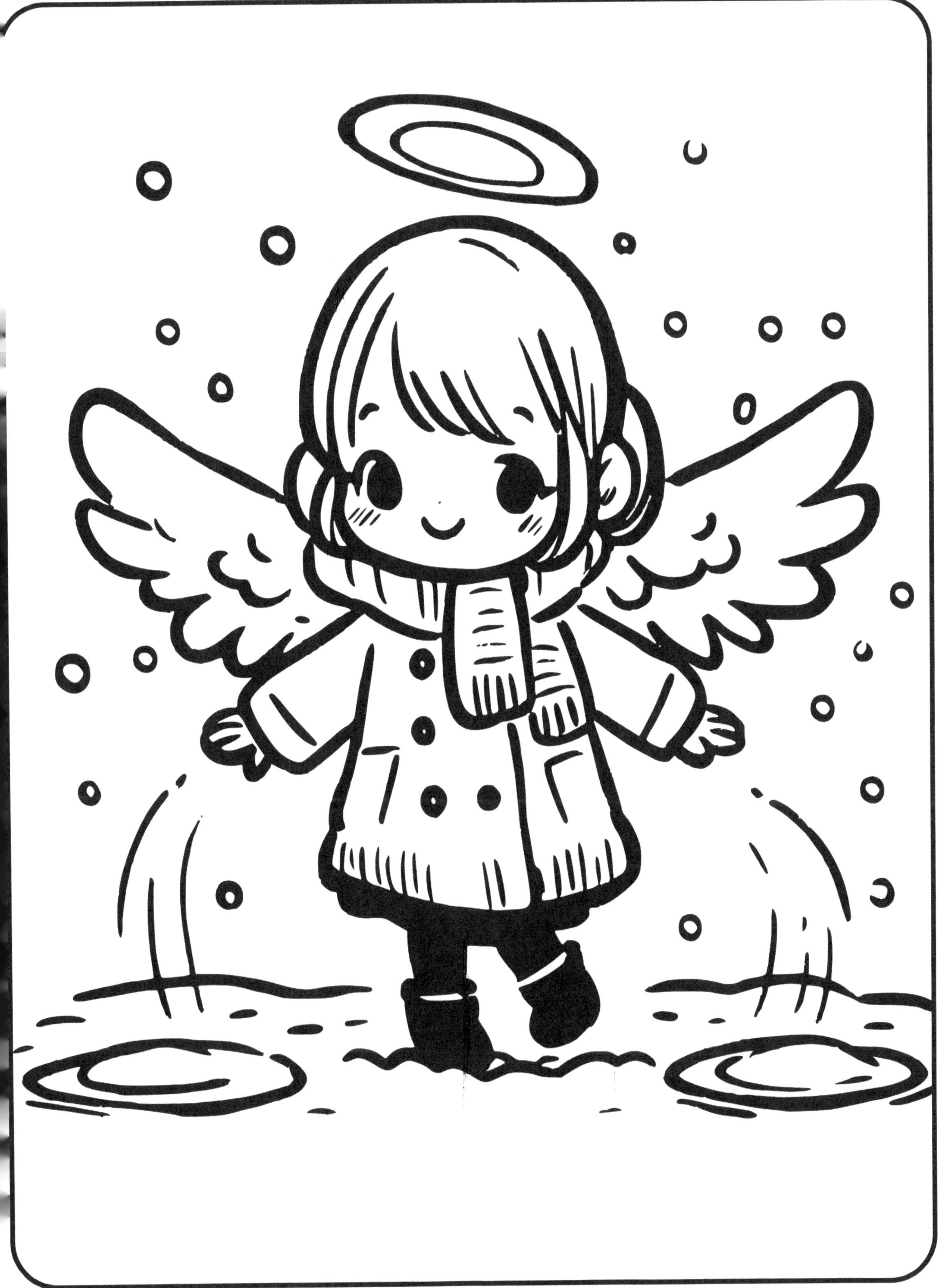

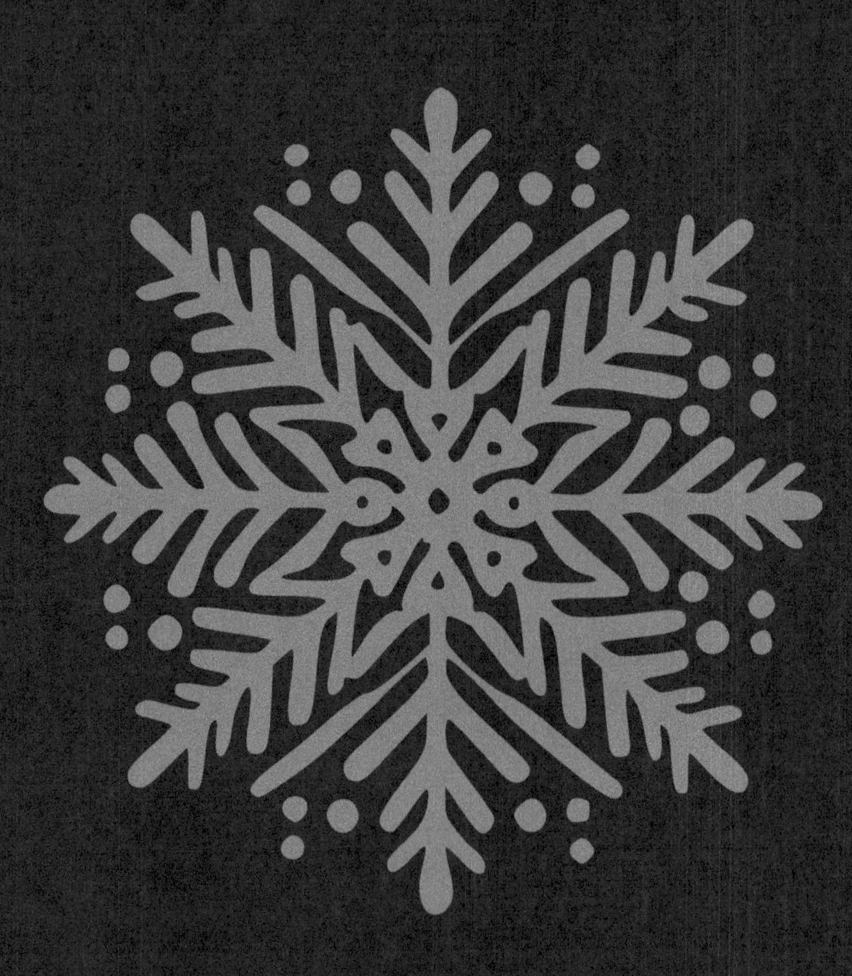

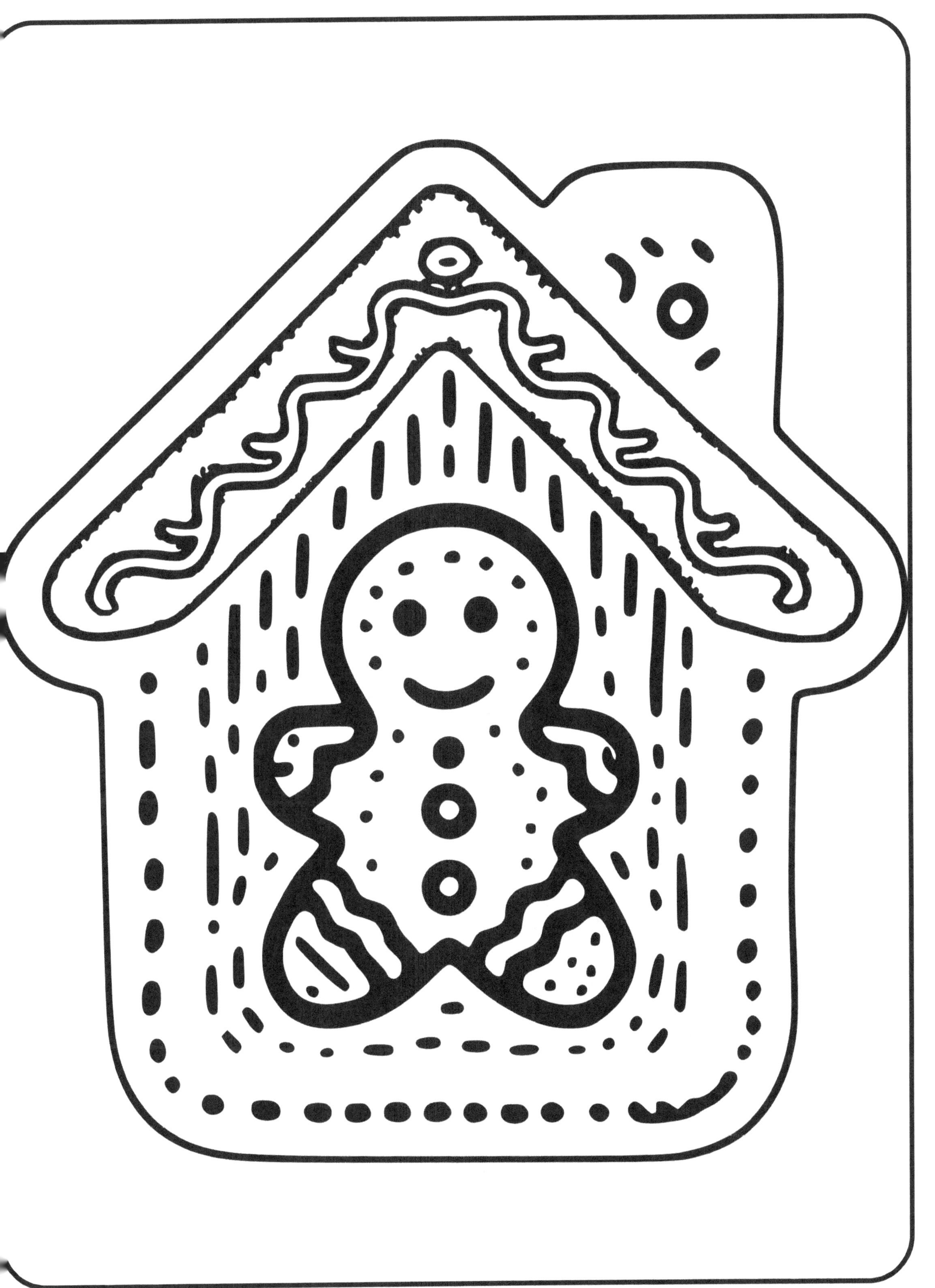

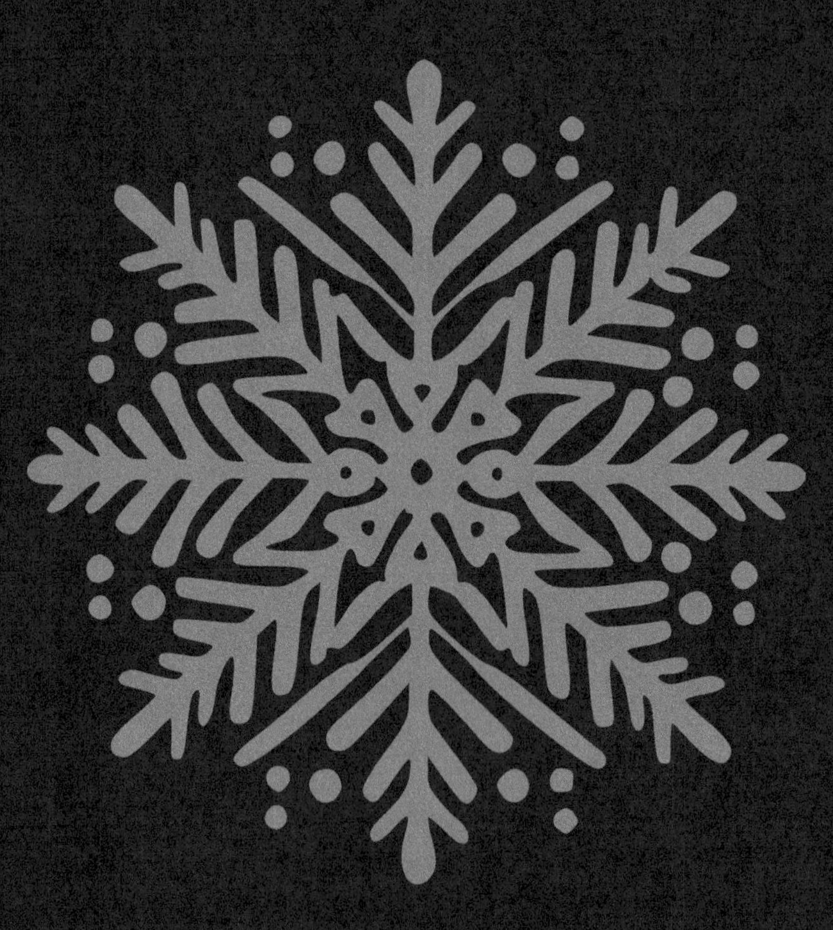

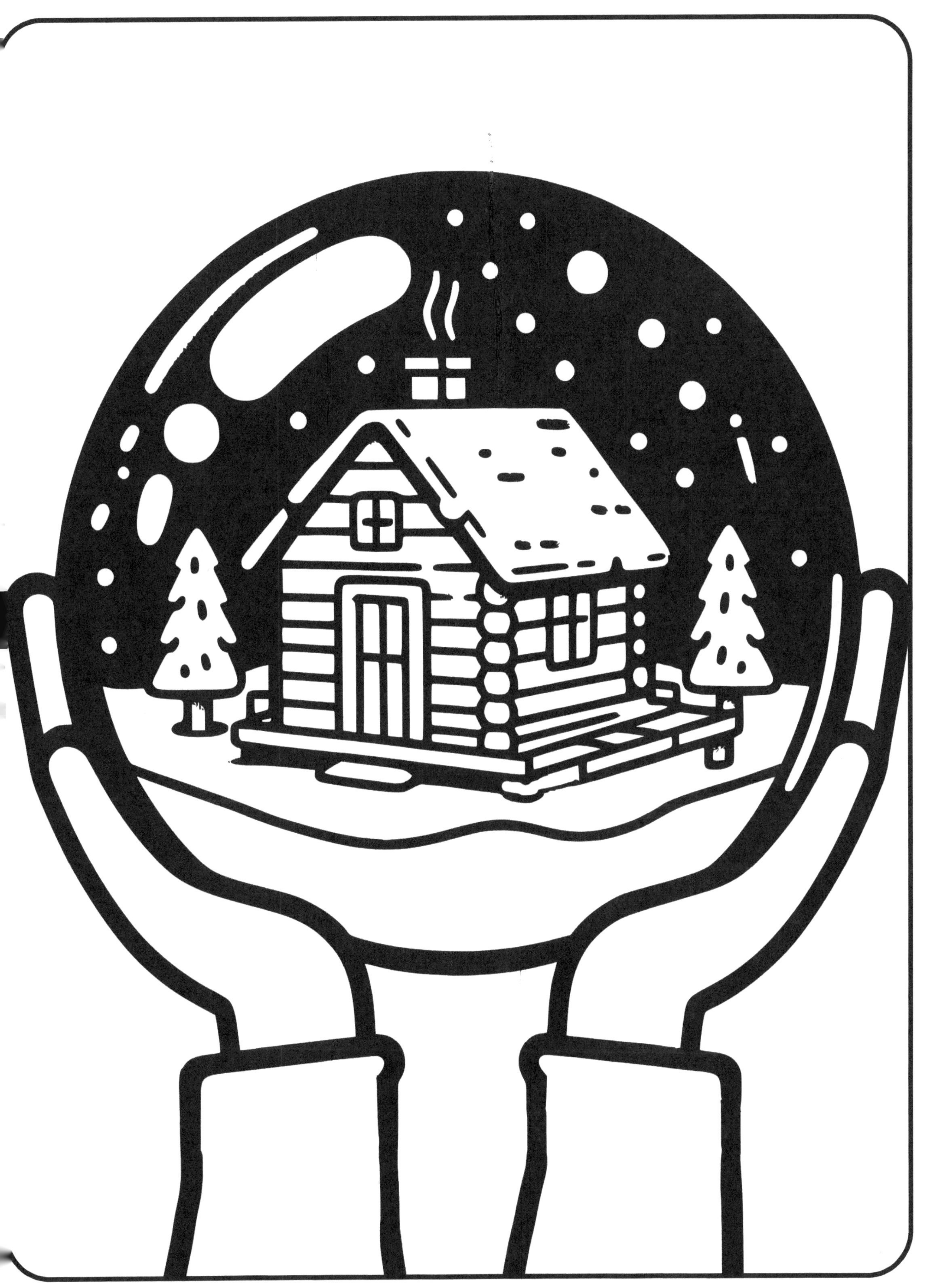

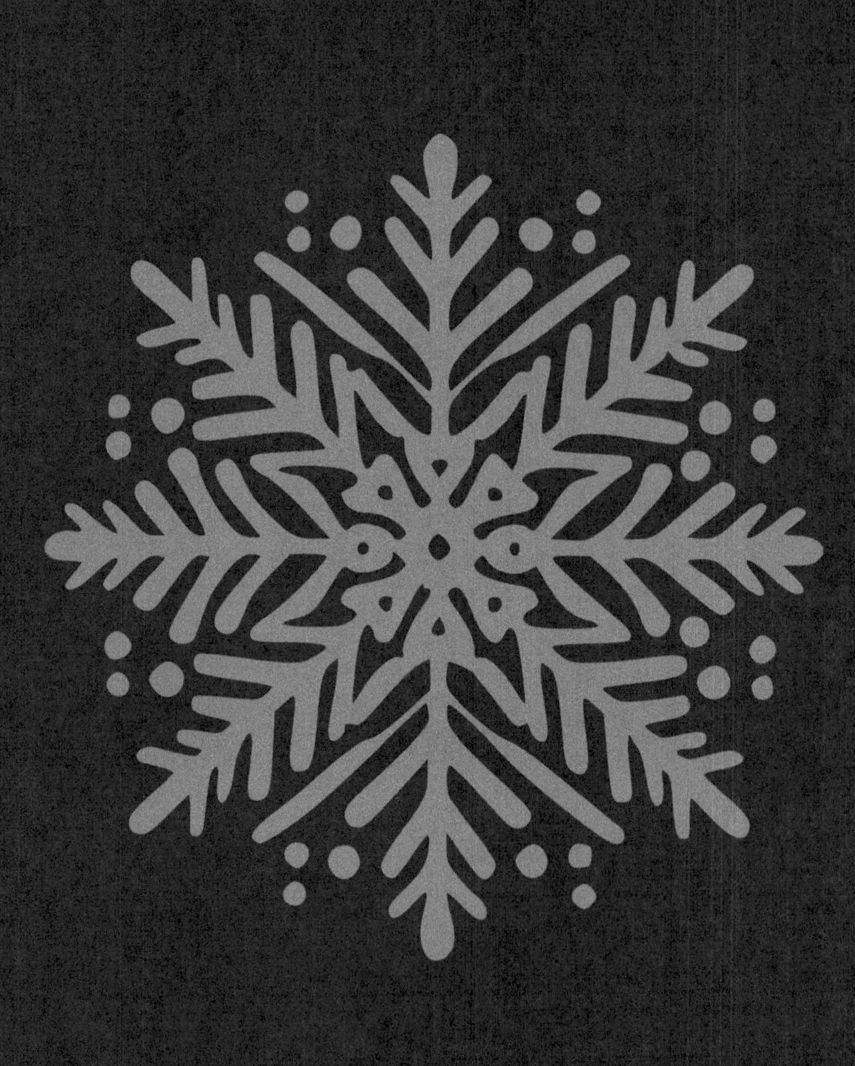

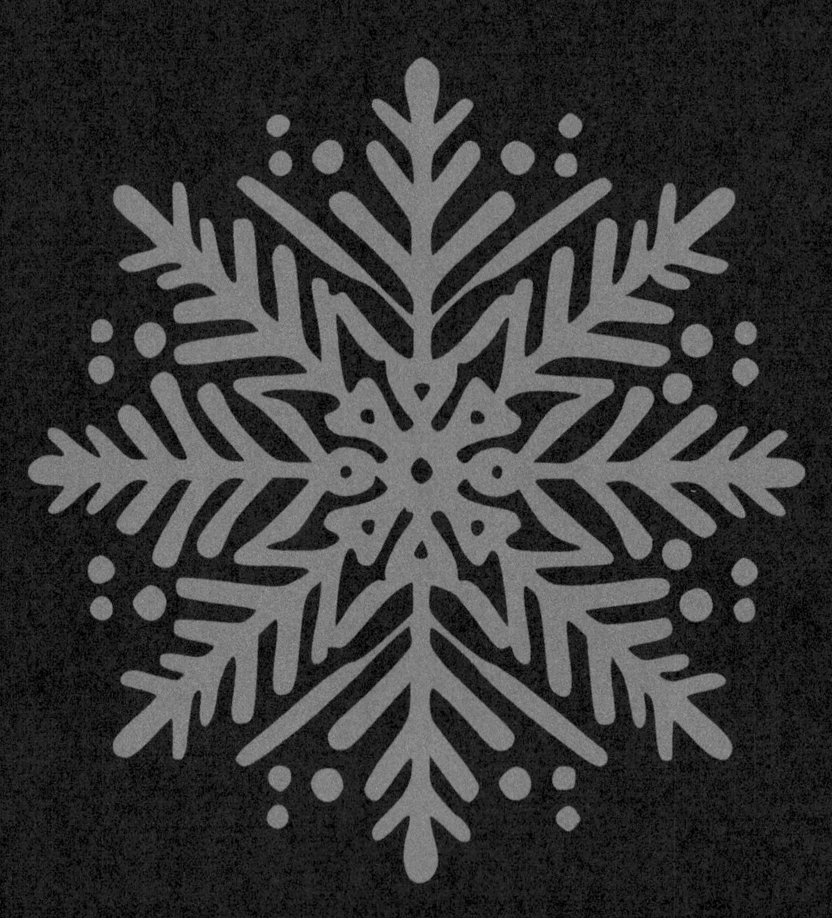

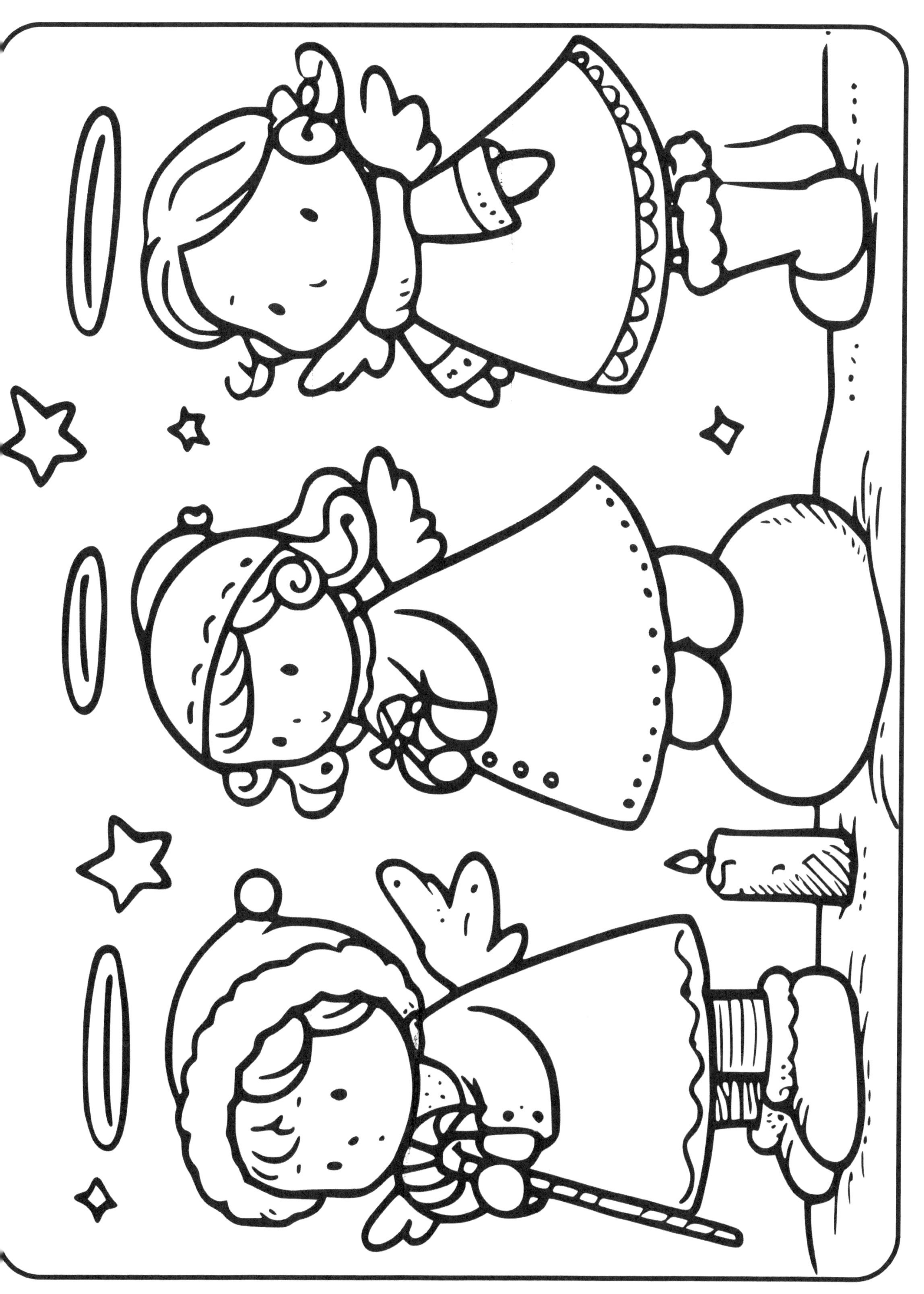

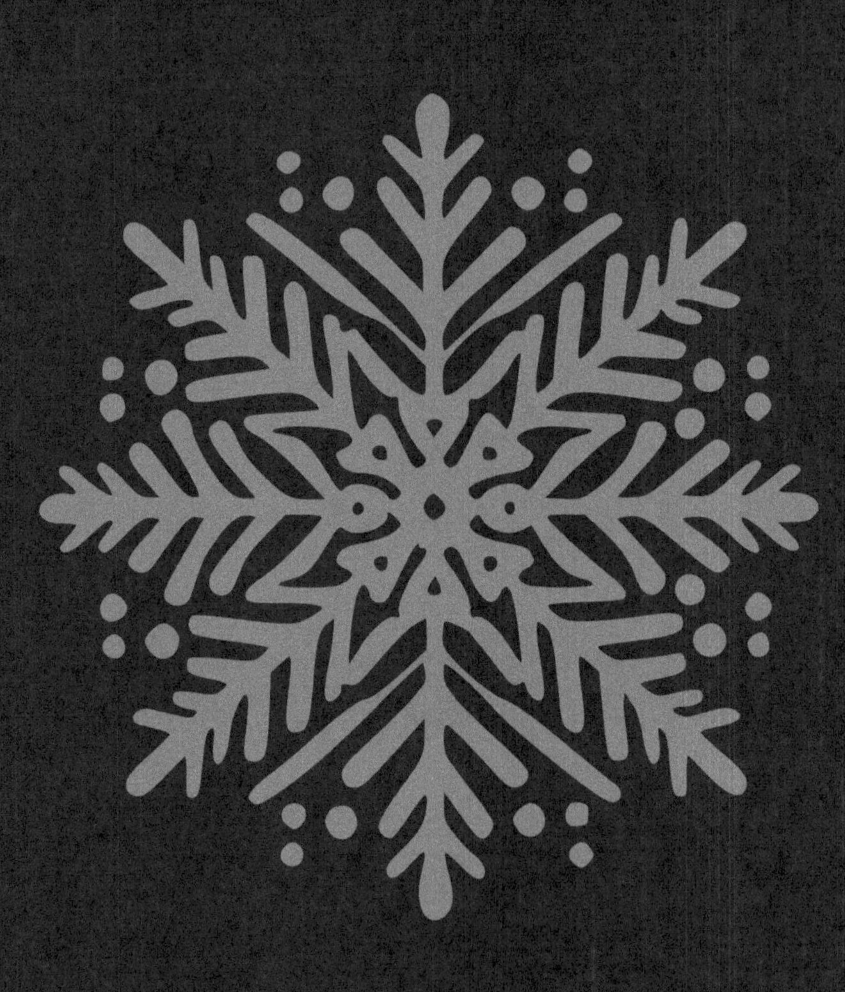

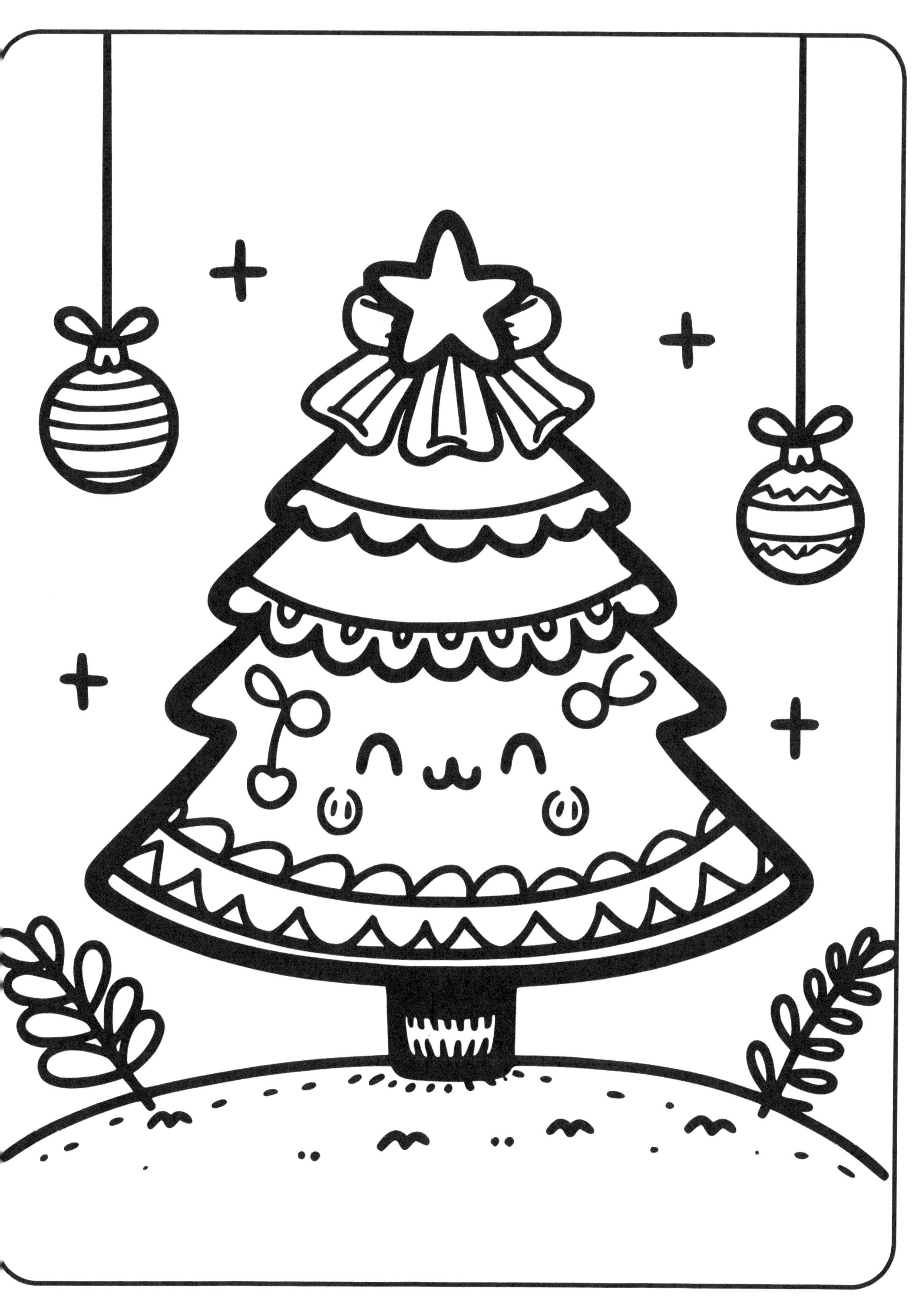

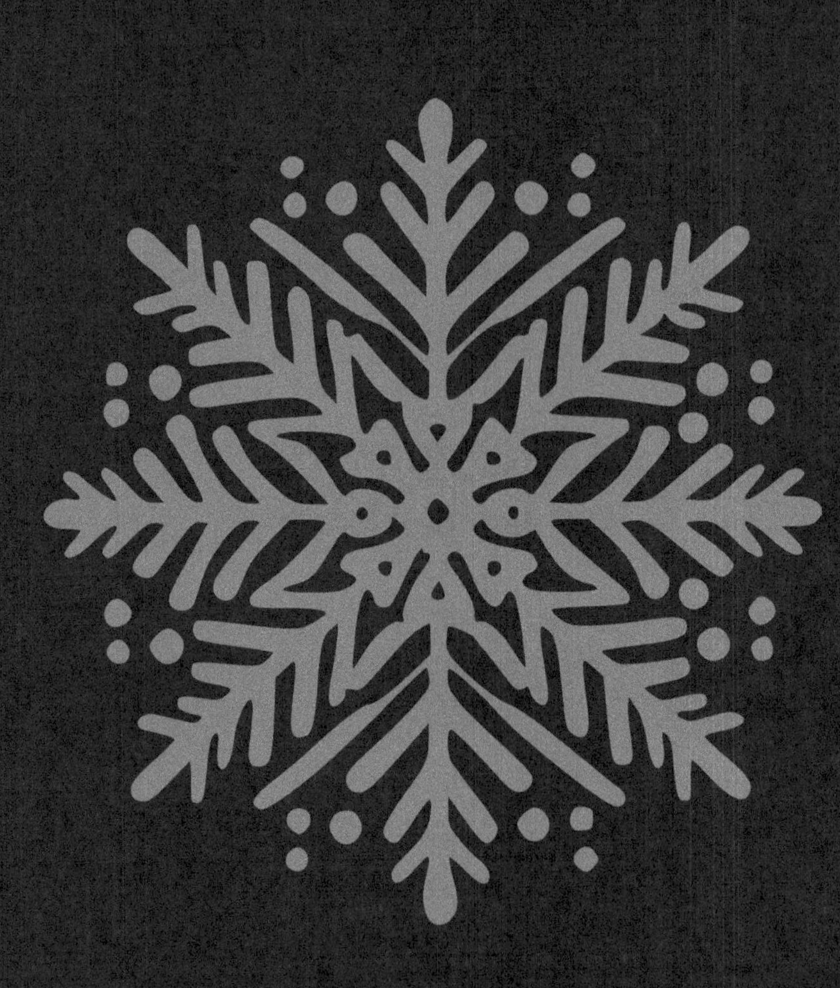

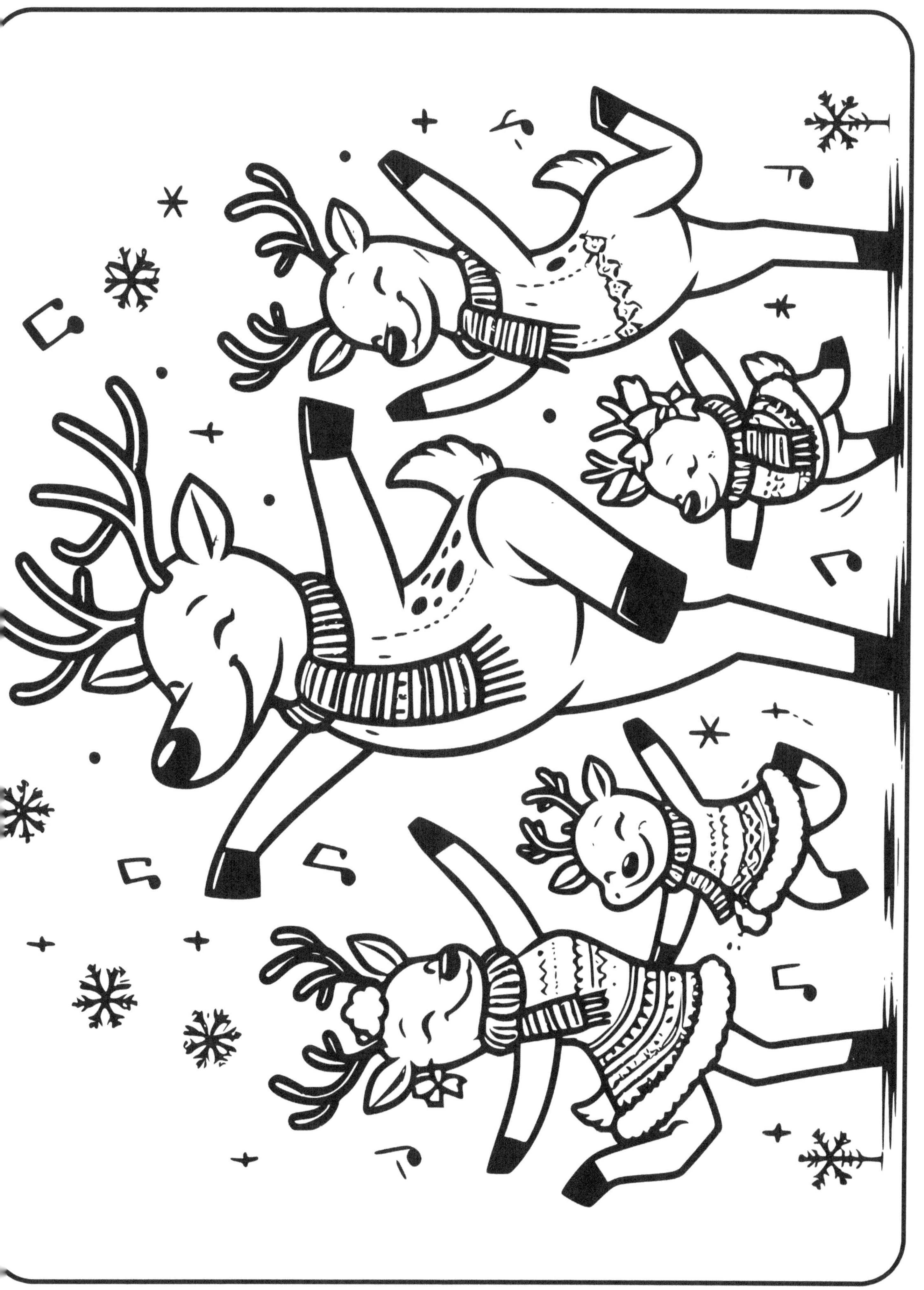

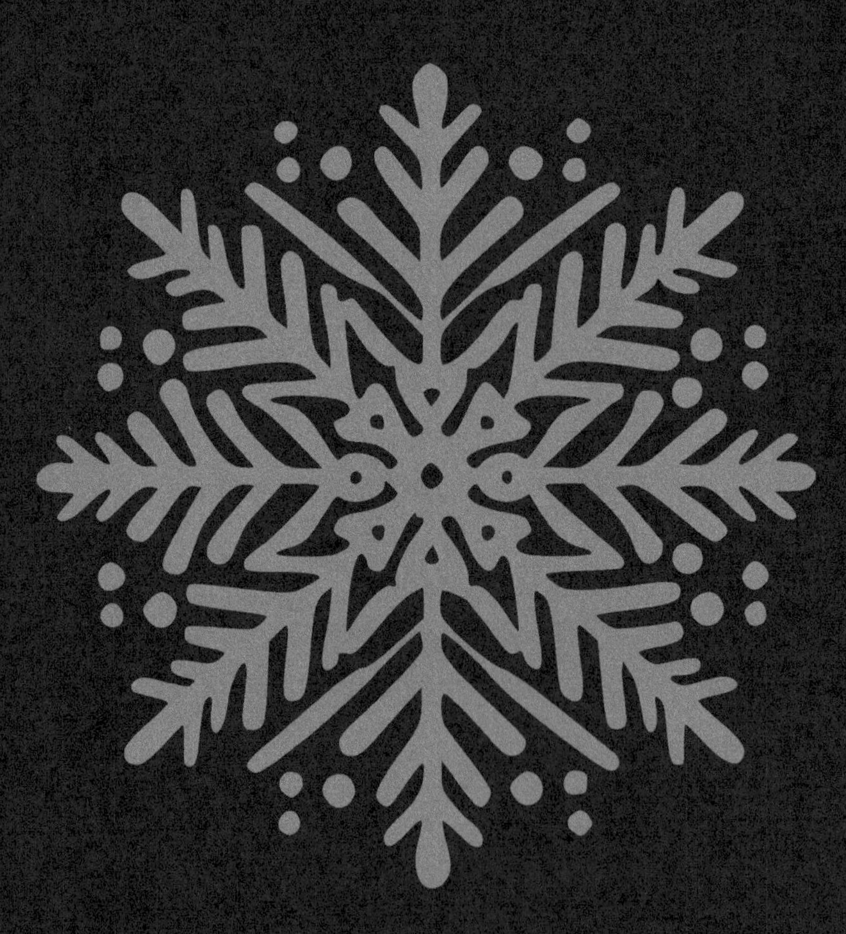

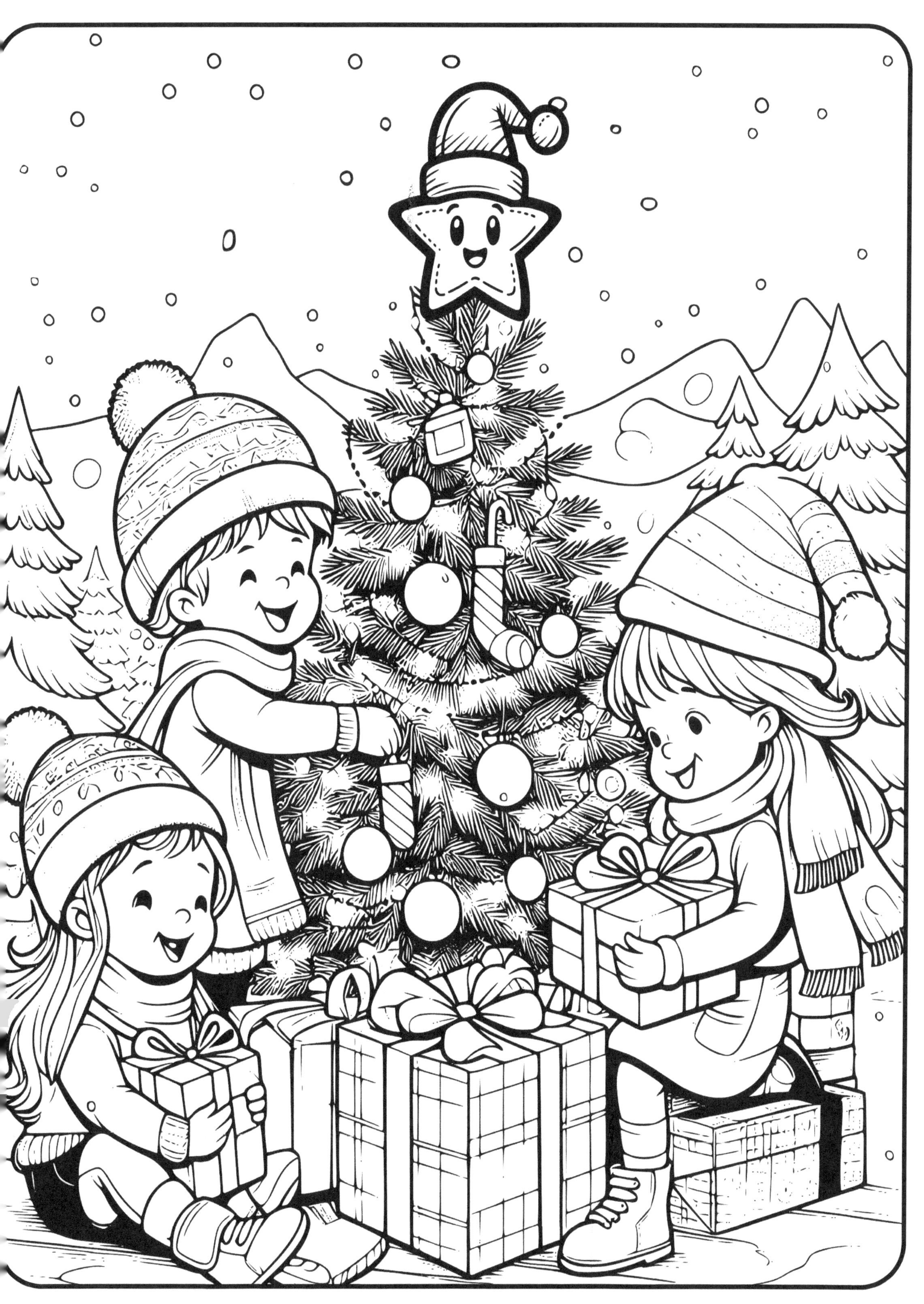

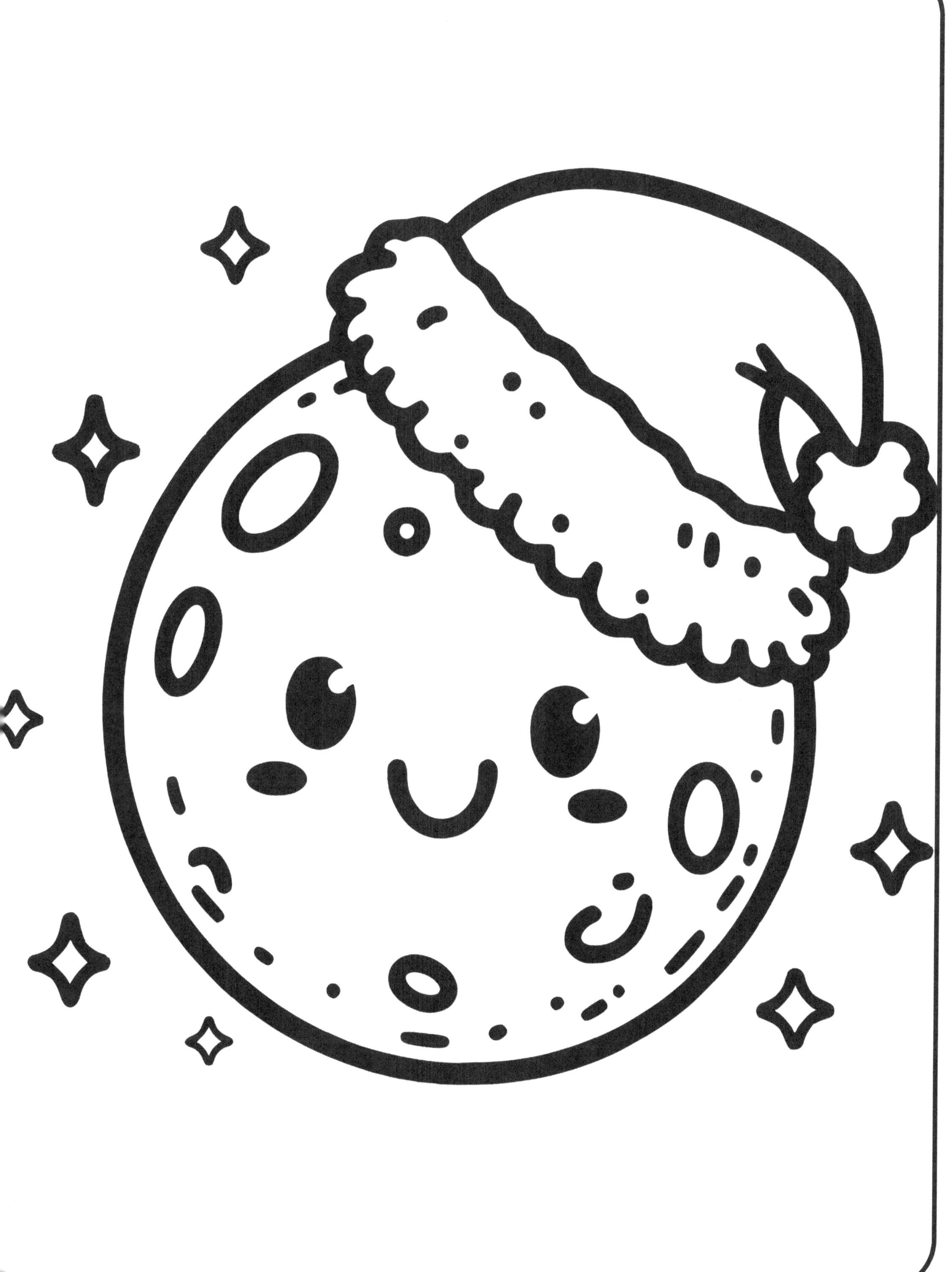

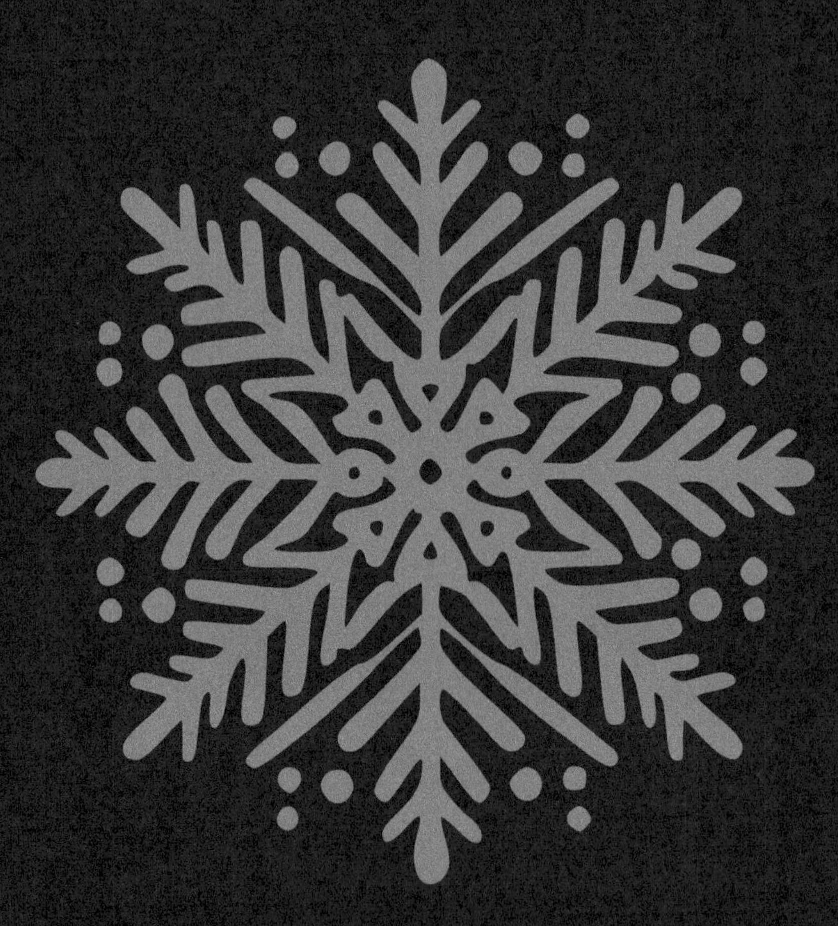

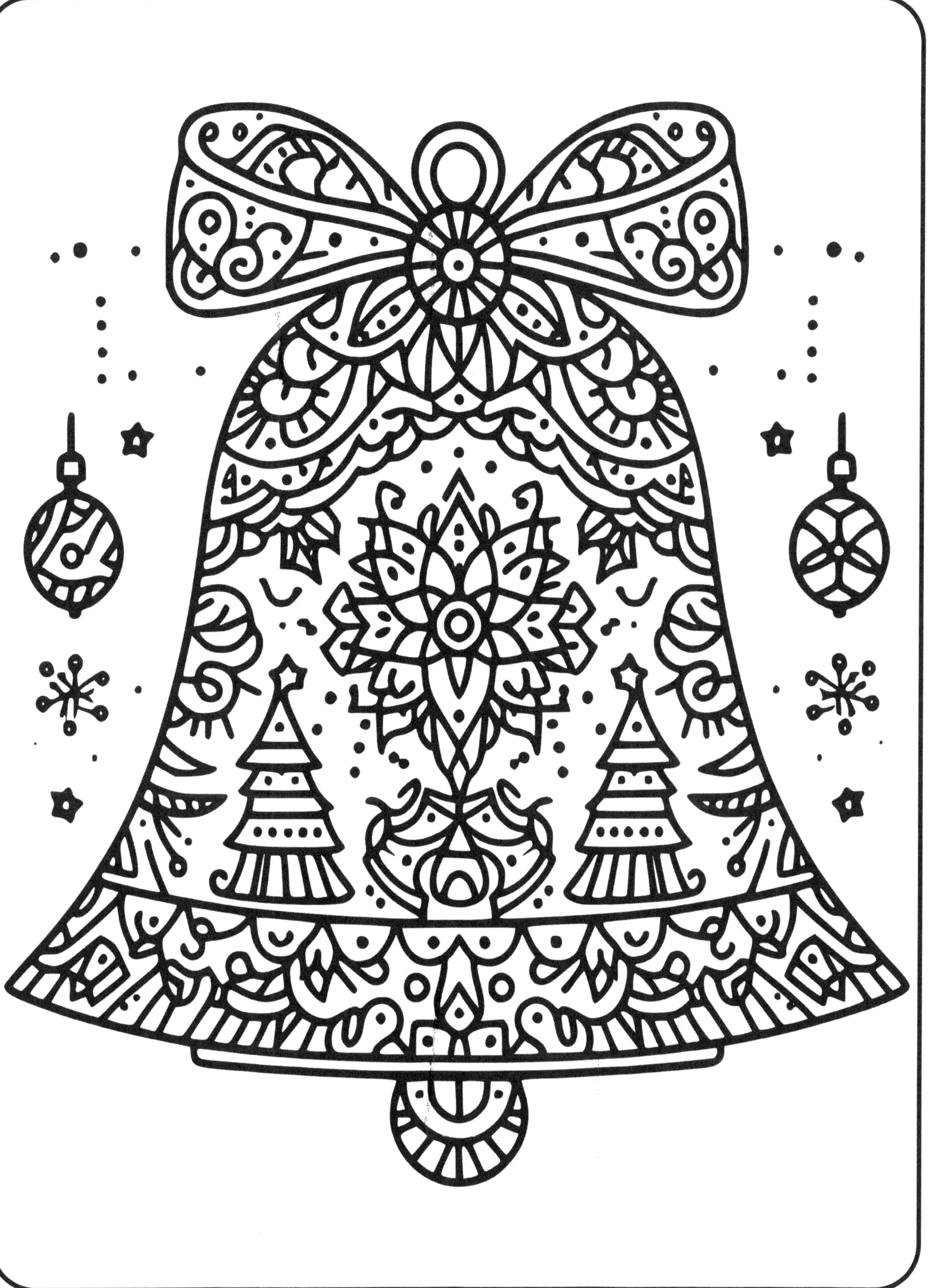

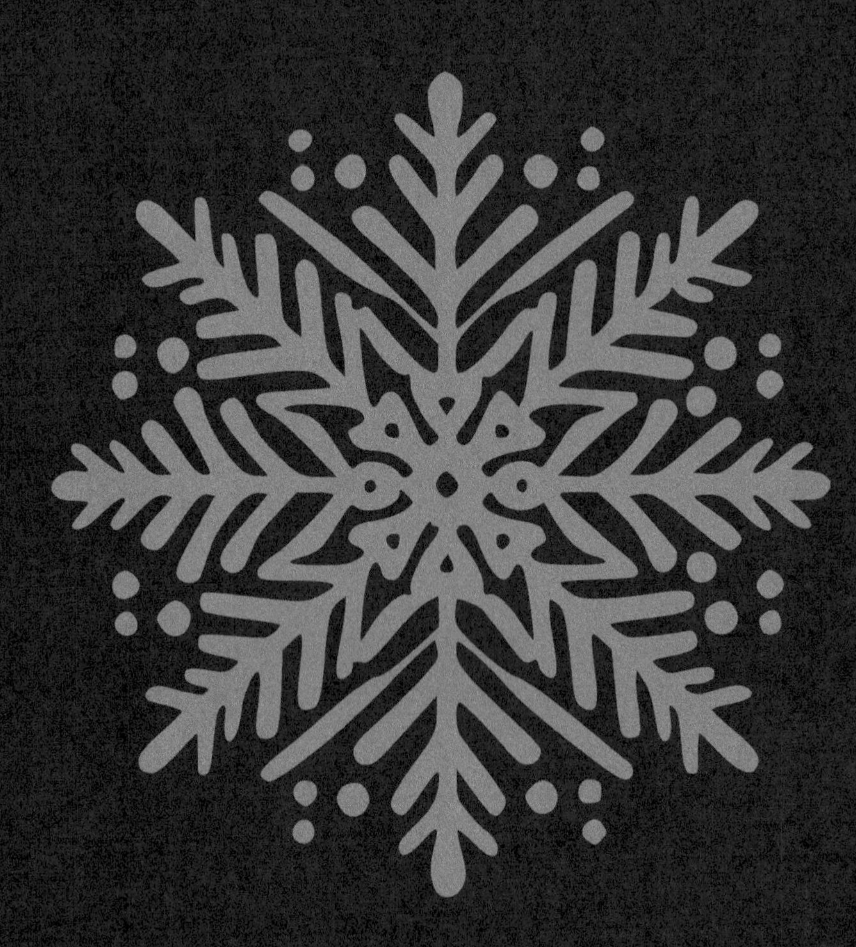

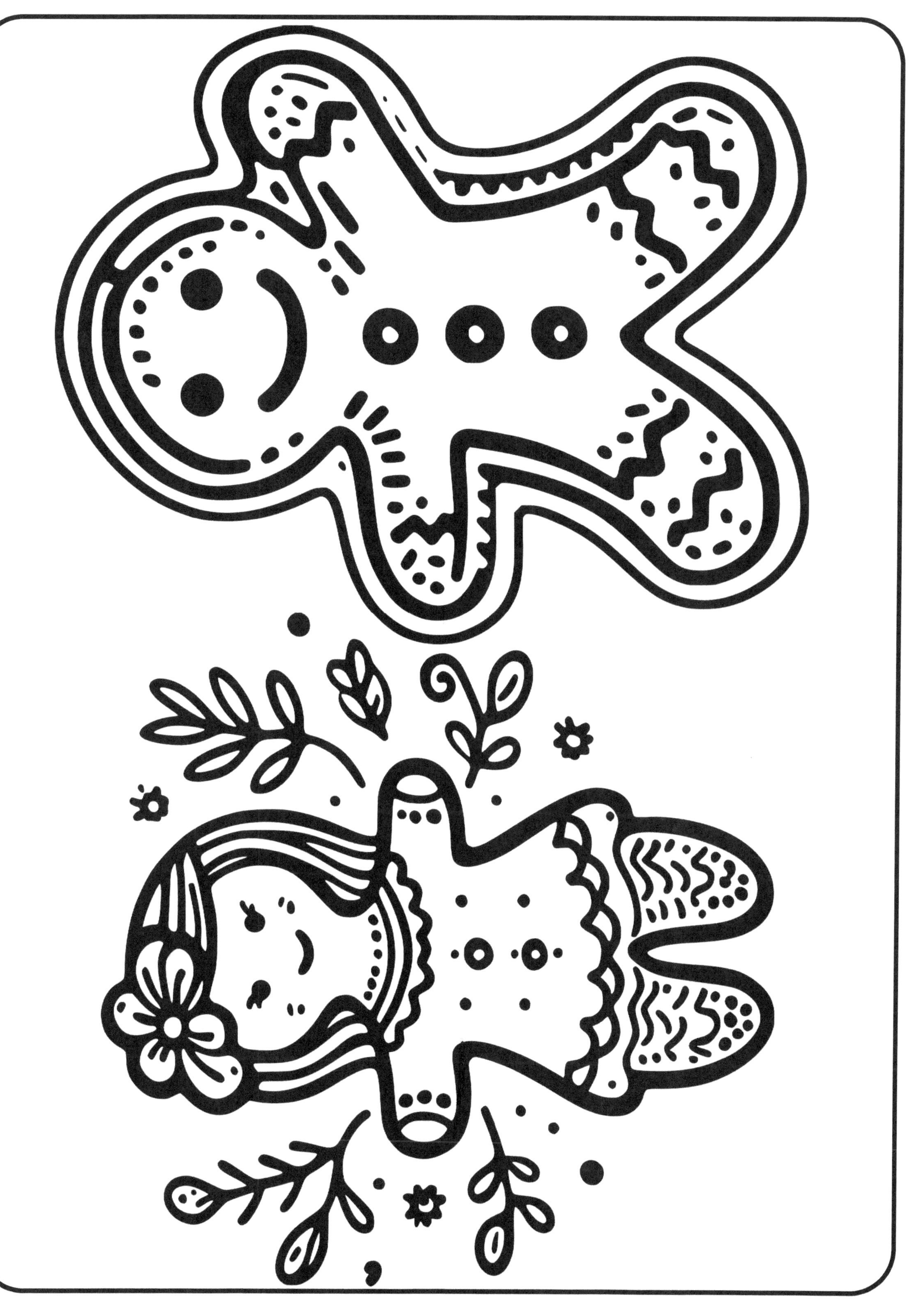

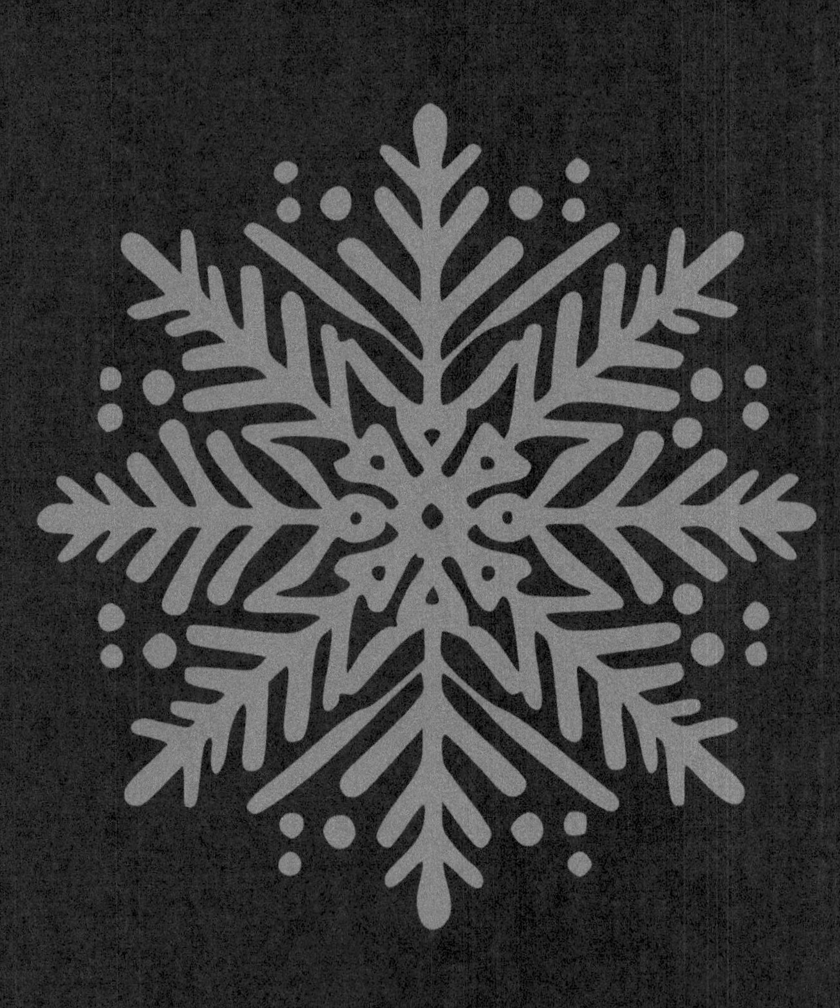

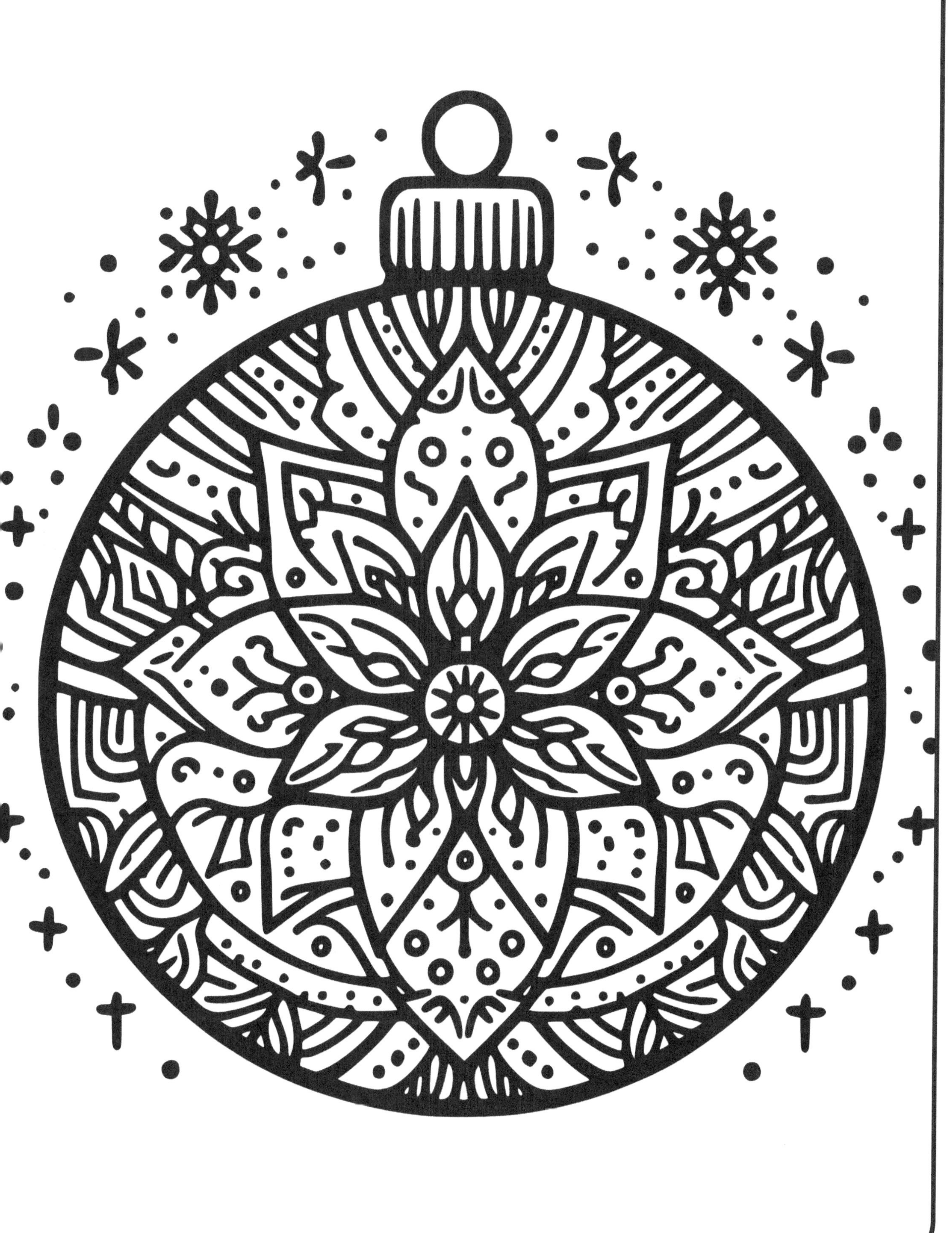

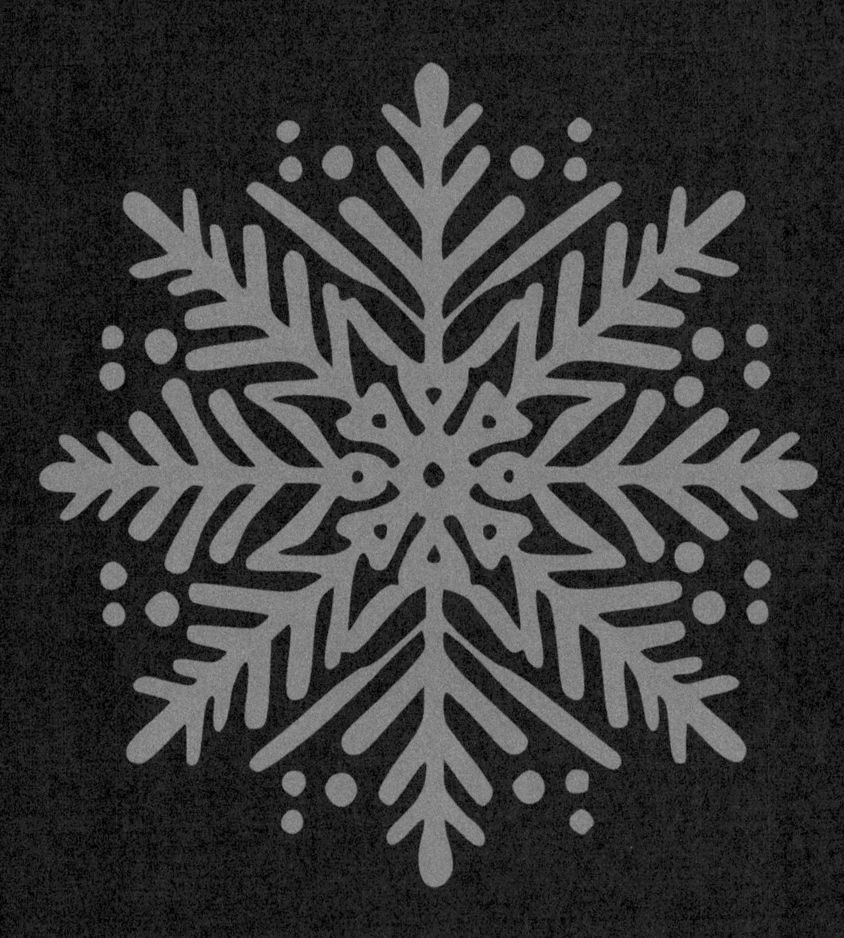

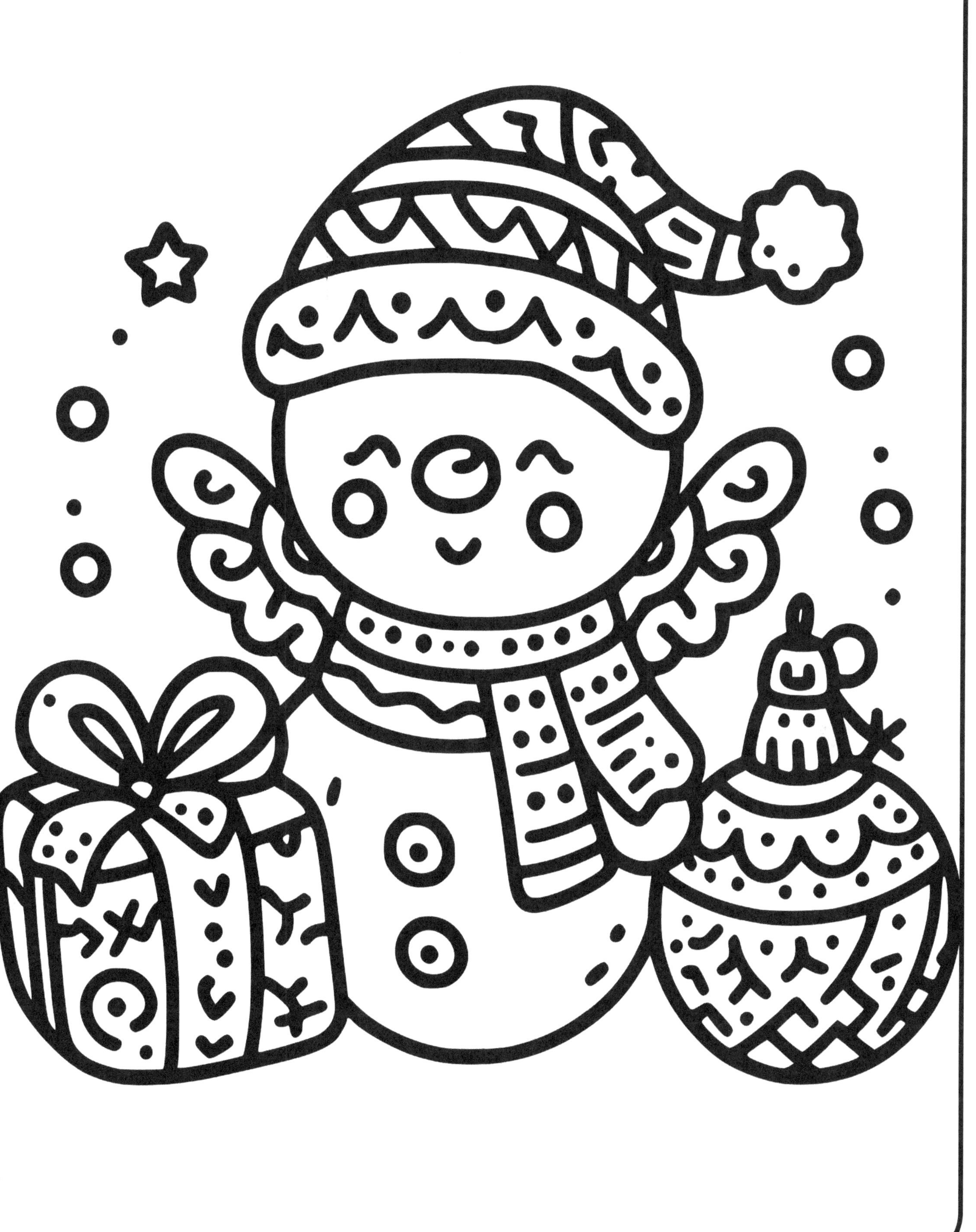

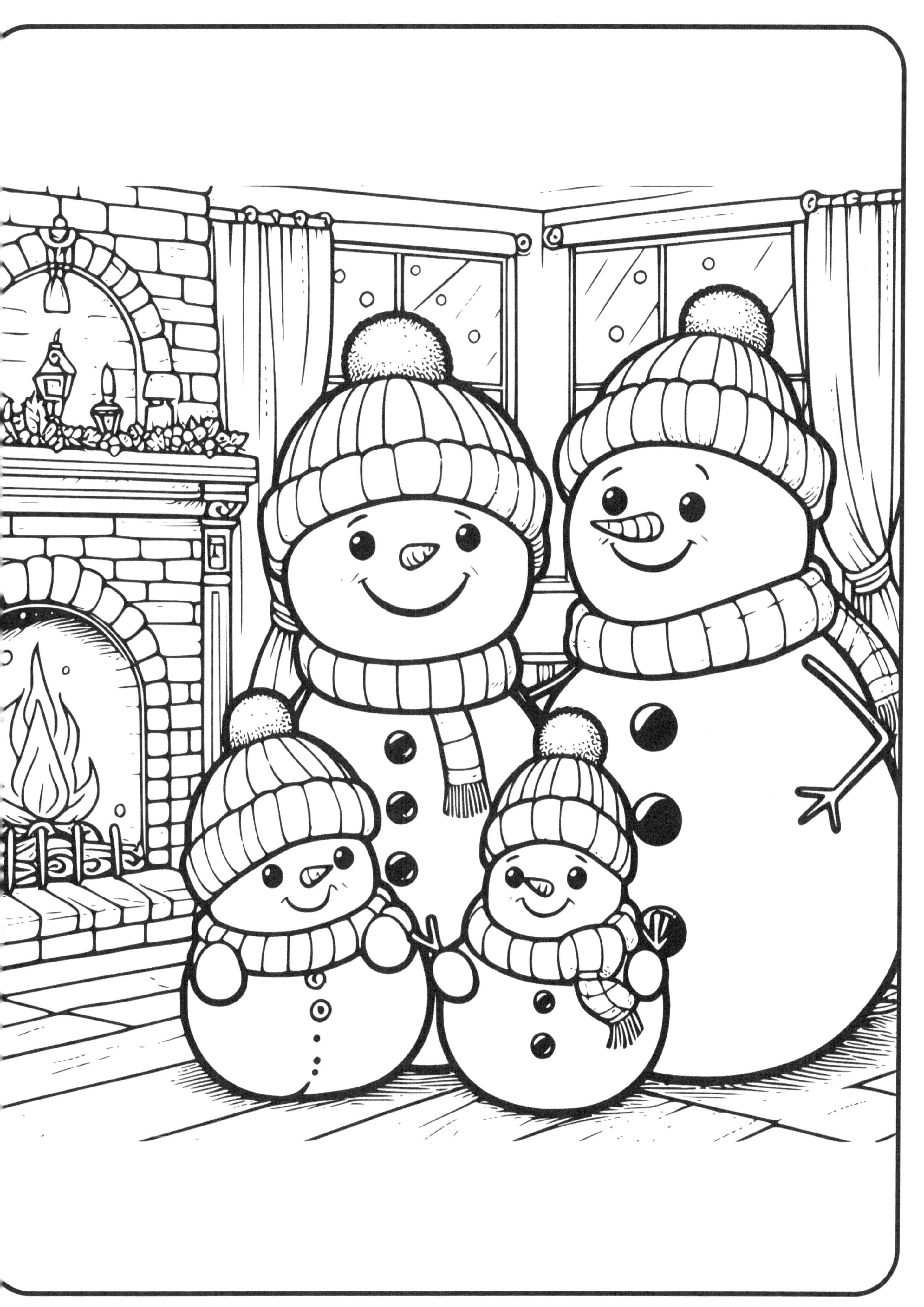

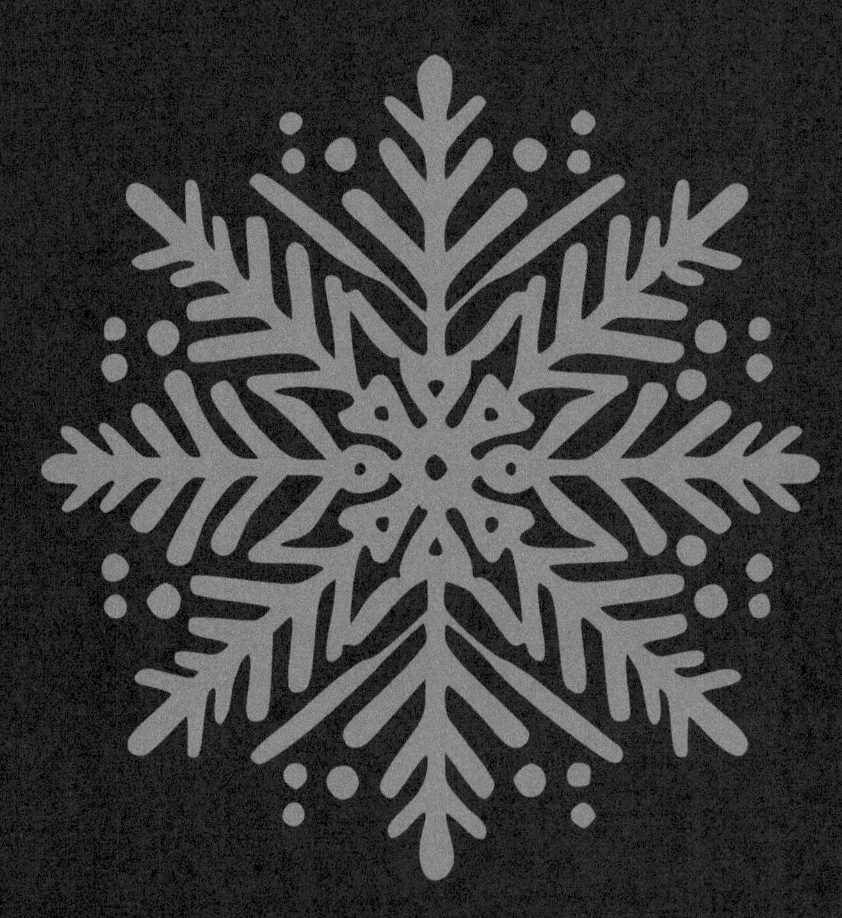

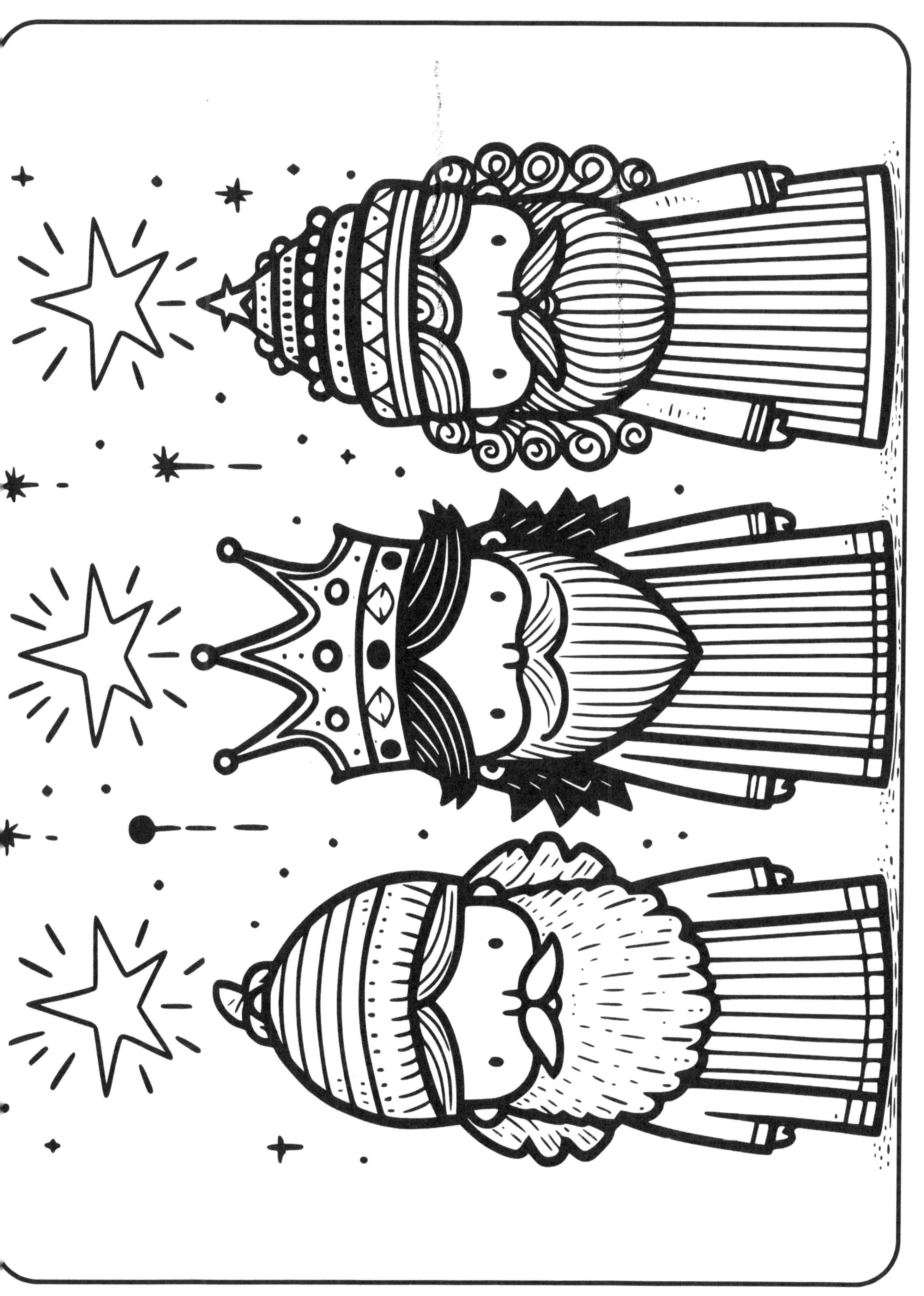

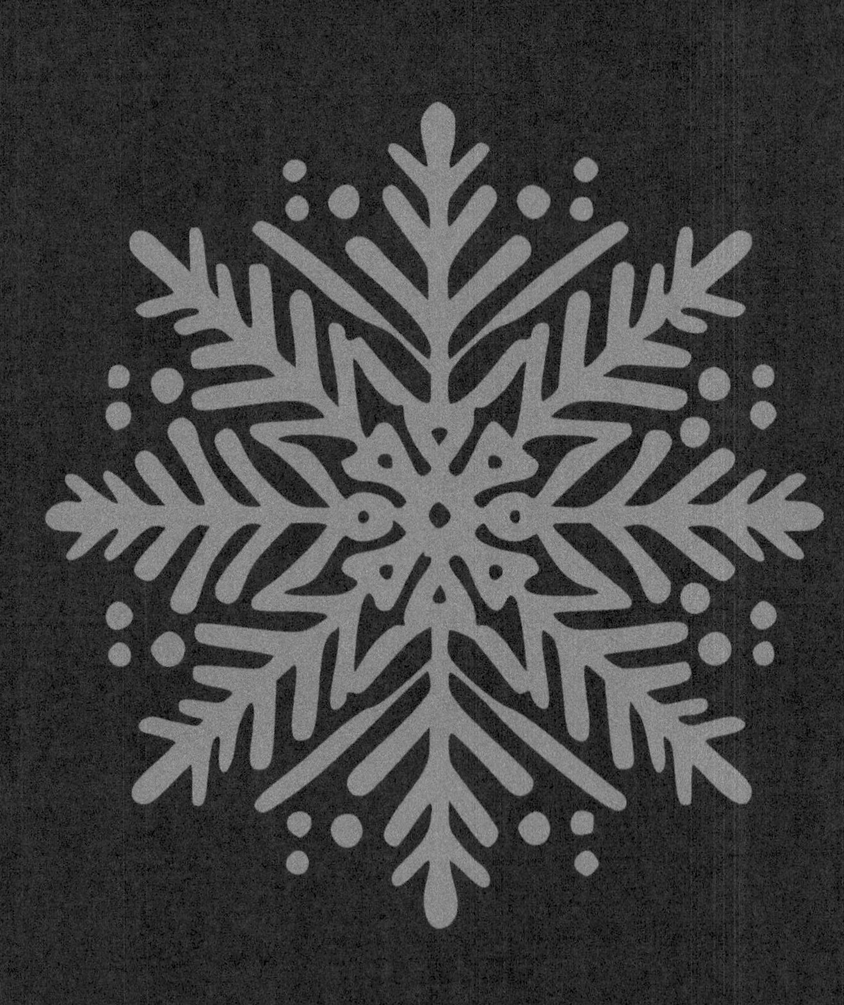